Michael Luck

Taoism
and
Ikigai

For beginners

A Complete Guide to Discover the Secrets of Taoist Philosophy and the Japanese Art for Finding Happiness and the Meaning of Life

Table of Contents

Michael Luck

Taoism

For beginners

A Complete Guide to Discover the Secrets of Taoism Religion and Taoist Philosophy

A Brief History Of Taoism

Taoism, a traditional Chinese religion dating back to 1800. in 2013, when master Zhang Taoling of the Eastern Han Dynasty (25-220) organized a religious Taoist group. Over the years of its development, Taoism has had a profound political, economic, cultural and ideological impact on ancient Chinese society and is still active.

During the Eastern Han Dynasty, Zhang Taolin moved to mount song Crane (Mount Heming). He claimed to have received " a powerful community of Orthodox unity (Zhengi Meng Wei) from Supreme Master Lao Ziho and began producing and distributing books promoting the Tao. His teachings focused on the calling of deities, magic and slavery, spirits and breathing exercises.

During the reign of Wei (220-265 A.D.), The Heavenly Master of Taoism created by Zhang Taolin was suppressed and rejected. However, when Zhang Lu and his students moved north of Hanjung, the heavenly master of Taoism began to be reborn in regions where Taoism of the highest level was already practiced. Then it spread throughout the country.

During the period of the Western Yin (265-316 A.D.) and the eastern Yin (317-420 A.D.), some families and influential scholars began to believe in Taoism. Taoism, which began at the grassroots level, has now infiltrated the upper class and over time has become an integral part of the spiritual life of the ruling class.

So, as more scientists turned to Taoism, the level of Taoist education increased. As a result, a vast set of Taoist scriptures was created that were supposed to provoke Indian Buddhism.

As the Taoist Scriptures spread, three new Taoist sects emerge: the Supreme purity (Shangqing), the divine treasure (Linbao), and the three August sects (Sanhuan).

In 589. in 2010, the Sui Dynasty (581-618) United China. At that time, several schools of Taoism began the process of integration. Masha's school, which evolved from a cult of high purity, became the dominant school in the south of the country and began to spread to the North. While Buddhism and Taoism practiced during the Sui Dynasty, Taoism developed rapidly, paving the way for this religion to reach its peak during the Tang Dynasty (618-907).

Li Yuan, founder of the Tang Dynasty, used public faith in Taoism a lot in the struggle to overthrow the Sui Dynasty. When he came to the throne, he announced that Lao Tzu, the founder of Taoism, was his ancestor (the surname is Lao Tzu-Lee and his name is ER). With the exception of Jetian (the only Empress in Chinese history), all emperors worshiped Tang Taoism.

The most influential development of Taoism during the period of the Five Dynasties (907-960) of late Taoism was the rise of the so-called inner alchemy created by Zhongli Quang and Lu Dongby..

Other schools of Taoism were born during the song, Yin and Yuan dynasties (960-1368 ad). Taoism has entered a new stage of development.

During the Northern Song Dynasty (960-1127 AD), the maoshan school still held a dominant position and its genre was very clear. The main new schools that emerged during this period were the sects of the heavenly heart (Tiankin) and the Divine Sky (Shenxiao).

In the Southern Song Dynasty (1127-1279), Taoism dominated the seven known as the mascot of the three mountains (Longhu Mountain, Maoshan and Gezao).

In addition, new sects such as Shenxiao, Donghua and Zingway were also active during this period.

In addition to the various old and new mascots, there were also pure light sects and Southern lines of the golden elixir of the sect during the Southern Song Dynasty.

The teachings of the supreme unity (Thaya), great Tao (Datao) and complete perfection (Quanzhen) at the end became the main forms of Taoism during the Jin dynasty (1115-1234.The doctrine of the higher unity lasted about 200 years and at the end of the Yuan dynasty was built in the tradition of the unity of the orthodox (Zhengyi). The Great doctrine of the Tao fell until the end of the yuan era and was also incorporated into the tradition of Orthodox unity. During the Yuan dynasty, perfection and tradition of Orthodox unity became the two main Taoist schools.

After the establishment of the Ming Dynasty (1368-1644 A.D.), Zhu Yuanzhang, the First Emperor of the Ming Dynasty, adopted a policy of Use and control of religion to preserve his property as the only dominant force in the country. As a result, Taoism began to fall.

Relatively speaking, the rulers of the Ming Dynasty preferred the tradition of Orthodox unity to the tradition of complete perfection. The first had a higher political status than the second. Zhu Yuanzhang believed that the sole purpose of meditation is practiced a cult full of excellence, it was the same meditation, while the tradition of

Orthodox unity maintained human relations and emphasized social customs, which played an important role in social stability. For this reason, he supported the tradition of Orthodox unity.

The rulers of the Qing dynasty (1644-1911 A.D.) believed in Tibetan Buddhism. They knew little about Taoism and therefore do not support or limit its development. The first emperors of the Qing dynasty followed the rulers of the Ming Dynasty and adopted a policy of defending Taoism because of the need to conquer Han China. But after the reign of Qianlong, the Qing rulers began to impose strict control over Taoism, leading to the fall of its political influence and stagnation of Organizational Development.

V. V., between the First Opium War (1840-1842) and the founding of the people's Republic of China in 1949.in the nineteenth century, China experienced a period of political chaos and the Chinese people suffered so much from the war and lived in great poverty.

Taoist buildings in the famous mountains fell into chaos and many Taoists left their temples. As a result, Taoism has become closely related to the everyday life of ordinary people. Initially, during the period of the Republic of China to settle in modern society, taoists tried to imitate the practices of western countries through the creation of national organizations to protect their interests. In 1912 he became one of the best. a national organization known as the central Taoist Association was founded in Beijing's white cloud temple, with a complete tradition of perfection as a backbone. At the same time, Zhang Yuanku, 23. The heavenly master who founded the Taoist Federation of the Republic of China in Shanghai, with the tradition of Orthodox unity as the basis. Both organizations were rather poorly organized and there were no significant events.

After China adopted a policy of reform and openness in 1979.in the XIX century, the Chinese Taoists continued the opening ceremony of the tradition of total perfection and the rules of transferring the mascot of the tradition of Orthodox unity.

In addition, extensive religious activities took place, such as a large ceremonial offering from the sky that surrounds everything. The Chinese Taoist school and Tao faculty in Shanghai to prepare a large number of priests, young and middle-aged; established academic institutes such as the Tao Cultural Research Institute of China and convened several forums in Tao culture; he founded journals such as Chinese taoism, Daoism, Tao, Taoism, Daoism, Taoism, Daoist, Taoism, Daoism, Taoism, Daoist, Taoism, Daoism, Taoism, Daoist, Taoism, Daoism, Taoism, Daoist, Taoism, Daoism, Taoism, Daoist, Taoism, Daoism, Taoism, Daoist, Taoism, Daoism, Taoism, Daoist, Daoism, Taoism, Daoist, Taoism, Daoism, Taoism, Daoist, Taoism, Daoism, Taoism, Daoist, Daoism, Taoism,

District-level governments approved about 1,500 Taoist monasteries to allow Taoists to participate in religious activities.

There are about 20,000 Taoist inhabitants full of traditions, perfection and tens of thousands of Taoist priests of traditions of Orthodox unity, as well as countless Taoist students throughout the country. An ancient religion has now turned into a real one. century with a completely new look.

Ritual

However, this belief in life for the development of the Tao does not belong to Taoist rituals. The rituals of Taoist practice fully correspond to Taoist understanding, but they are influenced by Buddhist and Confucian practices, so they are sometimes quite complex today. Every prayer and charm that is a Taoist ritual or festival must be accurately uttered, and every step of the ritual must be fully observed. A Taoist religious ceremony will be presided over by a Grand master (a kind of priest) who supports it, and these celebrations can last from a few days to more than a week. During the ritual, the Grand Master and his assistants must perform all the actions and recitations according to tradition, otherwise their efforts are useless. This is an interesting departure from the usual Taoist understanding of "flow tracking" and does not care about external rules or complex religious practices.

Taoist rituals aim to honor the ancestors of a village, community, or city, and the Grand master calls the spirits of these ancestor's incense to purify the area. Cleaning is a very important element throughout the ritual. The shared space of everyday life should be transformed into a sacred space for communication with spirits and gods. There are usually four assistants who help the grandmaster in different titles, whether they are musicians, Saint dancers, or readers. The Grand master interprets the text as read by one of his assistants, and this text refers to the elevation of the soul to join the gods and his ancestors. In ancient times, this was a ritual that took place on the stairs leading to the altar to symbolize the ascent of its common environment to the greater ascent of the gods. The ritual can currently be performed on stage or on the floor, and this is heard with the text and actions of the great riding master.

The altar still plays an important role in the ritual, as it is perceived as the place where the earthly Kingdom meets the divine. Taoist families have their own altar where people will pray and respect their ancestors, household spirits, and the spirits of their village. Taoism requires individual worship at home, and rituals and festivals are social events that bring people together, but should not be equated with the practice of worshipping other religions, such as going to Church or temple. Taoists can adore homes without even attending a festival, and throughout their history, most people have. Festivals are very expensive on stage and are usually funded by members of a town, village, or city. They are usually considered social holidays, but sometimes they are performed when necessary, such as an epidemic or financial struggle. Ghosts and gods are currently attractive for driving the dark spirits that are causing the problem.

Taoism strongly influenced the Chinese culture of the Shang dynasty. The recognition that all things and all people are connected is expressed in the development of art that reflects an understanding of their place in the Universe and their mutual obligations. During the Tang dynasty, Taoism became the state religion during the reign of Emperor Xuanjong, as he believed that it created a harmonious balance in his subjects, and after a while, he was right. The reign of Xuanzong is still considered one of the most prosperous and stable in Chinese history and the culmination of the Tang dynasty.

Taoism has been called state religions several times in Chinese history, and the teachings of the most beloved Confucius (or, sometimes, Buddhism), most likely because of the rituals of those beliefs that provide the Taoist structure, are not enough. Today, Taoism is recognized as one of the largest religions in the world and is still practiced by people in China and around the world.

Is Taoism a Religion?

Often the question of Taoism is whether it is a religion.

The answer you will get depends on who you are talking about.

Taoism was actually practiced as a religion. Around many Taoists. For example, many Southeast Asian Chinese were born Taoists, but not necessarily religious. I'm one of them.

Since it is practiced as a religion, a religious Taoist will give you an affirmative answer.

However, there is something interesting about Taoism as a religion: do not think that when Christ knows Jesus Christ and the Bible, the Taoist of course knows Lao Tzu-the founder of Taoism-and his text is more visible by The Tao Te Jing.

The question is " what do you do as a Taoist?" this can generate a number of responses. The Taoists go to the temples to pray to the gods. But they do not necessarily pray Lao Tseu. They worship deities of religious figures such as Guanyin, historical figures such as Guanyu or legendary figures such as monkeys, which are not necessarily related to Taoism. Lao Tzu, or better known as Taishang Laojun, is only one. And the fans don't care.

In fact, you will be surprised to learn that many religious Taoists do not know Lao Tseu, not to mention the quotes from Tao Jing's poems. They will probably tell you things like respect for the son, personal honesty and justice, which is a fusion of Chinese culture and not a Lao-Tse thought.

From this point of view, I would consider Taoism or as a reflection of Chinese culture rather than religion.

It is equally interesting that many who read Lao Tzu and speak of Tao are not called Taoists. They teach the Tao Qing to understand the universe and practice Tao as a way of life. But they do it philosophically, not religiously. There are also those who practice the activities of Tao, meditation,

Qigong to Tai-Chi, and who do not even know that the activity is related to Tao.

If you asked these people, is Taoism a religion? We would say that this is not the case.

So, back to the question, is Taoism a religion?

I can conclude that there are two ways to pursue Taoism. One is religious, the other is not. The religious approach guides Taoism through religious rituals such as burning joss ' wands and giving deities. Non-religious consider this a philosophy and study the teachings of the sages as a way of life.

Among the Chinese, those who consider Taoism as a religion describe Taoism as Tao Jiao (it can be translated by the domain of Tao); and those who consider it as a philosophy describe it as Tao Jia (School of thought of Tao).

Therefore, the answer to the question of whether Taoism is a religion is yes and no.

As a passionate reader gave you Jing, I can not find a book to be religious at all. In fact, it wasn't supposed to be a religious text when it was first written. It was part of the rich intellectual heritage of the Chinese military period around the 4th century BC - an era of dynamic cultural and intellectual development in ancient China.

Why Is Taoist Tai Chi So Popular?

Taoist Tai Chi is a mixture of Taoism and Tai Chi Chuan. It is a more comprehensive approach than any of them, because it works both on your mind and body. It has evolved as a holistic approach to health and wellbeing and combines both approaches into uniform practice.

Tai Chi Chuan, translated as the ultimate Fist, is a practice developed for defense and its health benefits, so it focuses more on improving the body. Taoist practices are a number of philosophical and religious beliefs that evolved in ancient India and China.

Here's what you need to know...

1 this practice has its roots in martial arts and Taoism, the set of philosophical traditions and beliefs, which emphasize moderation, compassion and harmony.

2: it is a great practice for your mind and body. Her doctors claim that these health benefits:

* Stretching aspects improve the function of ligaments, tendons and joints.

* It is an exercise in weight and as such can help maintain bone density.

* Taoist forms of Tai-Chi stimulate the spinal nerves, which leads to a balanced effect on the nervous system.

* Long stretches reduce muscle tension.

* By relaxing the mind while exercising, the brain requires less energy and stress levels are reduced.

* Helps regulate the immune system.

3: helps you escape the stress of our modern life. For the correct practice of art, it is necessary to calm the mind, which is easier said than in our modern society. You need to move away from worries, doubts and tasks to your basic nature of peace, compassion and peace.

Taoist Tai Chi Society is a dynamic nonprofit organization with over 40,000 members in 26 countries. Their task is to bring benefits to everyone. The company is very popular in Canada and is growing rapidly. Some chapters offer courses aimed at recovery for those who have special needs.

If you're serious about improving your overall health, you should definitely try some Taoist tai Chi exercises. If you feel better and more relaxed, it can be very useful in everyday practice for you. In recent years have been created many high-quality DVD programs, to teach them basic exercises and the philosophy behind the art of Taoist Tai Chi. These programs can help you get started with the basics before looking for professional guidelines.

Chinese Taoist Wisdom for the Modern Day

The Yin / Yang symbol is one of the oldest and most famous symbols in the world, but few people understand its meaning. Although it is widely used in fashion and media, it is actually an ancient Chinese symbol expressing a deep philosophy. It represents two opposite but complementary pillars of existence that exist in everything. Yin represents everything that is feminine, dark, uplifting, receptive and passive, and things that go down and in. Yang is masculine, bright, strong and expansive, and Moving up.

According to the philosophy, everything contains Yin and Yang, so we see a white spot in the black segment of the Yin / Yang symbols and Vice versa. In fact, when something happens to the extreme, it always happens to its opposite. This is illustrated in nature in many ways, but it applies to all things: a storm precedes and follows a great calm, cold replaces heat, which replaces cold in a constant cycle of seasons; too strict an organization will cause a rebellion when the rules are too strict; a bubble will burst if it is overestimated.

These examples seem trivial, but a person who can see how Yin and Yang work in the world can predict the outcome of an event. Therefore, the ancient Chinese Taoists recognize that everything is constantly changing, moving first in one direction and then in another. Modern Taoists always try to use this principle and, among other things, can help reduce stress without feeling anxious or anxious when obstacles or difficult times, knowing that everything will improve.

- The key is in balance. Neither extreme Yin nor extreme Yang is usually very good. In all aspects of life, being between extremes usually makes running smoother and less stressful. For example, someone who is very motivated and always works and is in a hurry is too young and will soon burn out. Again, a teledipendent who never leaves TV and has no goals or ambitions is too Yin and may also suffer from poor health and depression. The half between these two extremes is lighter and healthier.

Yin and Yang are used in many Chinese arts and disciplines. -

In traditional martial arts and tai Chi movements, they constantly expand and then come together, and practitioners are encouraged to stay in extreme positions so as not to get out of balance. In Chinese medicine, diseases and medicines are classified as Yin and Yang, and even Chinese cuisine considers these 2 properties of different foods and tries to balance Yin and Yang in food!

Thus, for the ancient Chinese and those around the world today who adhere to Taoist discipline, Yin and Yang are not abstract ideas, they are part of the whole world and everything they do. By understanding, looking and waiting for the influence of Yin and Yang, Taoism can bring a better balance to your life. In these stressful times, these old ideas are as important as they were thousands of years ago, if not more!

A Quick Guide to Taoist Meditation

The daily stress and anxiety you experience at work and in your personal life are many causes of mental and physical stress; this condition can be greatly relieved by practicing the art of Taoist meditation.

Choosing Taoist meditation is a choice for creating, tuning, and directing energy into an orbit in you. When a person reaches this energy, they can use it to improve their life. The energies of the body, emotions, and mind are used to solve problems and achieve a higher level of spirituality. With these advantages, artists will have a more peaceful and peaceful existence.

Taoist meditation explains two basic principles: Jing and Ding. The first principle, I Ching, is interpreted as peace, silence, and silence. Its goal is to move away from external forces in the mental and physical sense and draw all attention to internal self-confidence. Thus, a person is able to control the "five thieves": eyes, ears, nose, tongue, and body. Each of these "thieves "can say goodbye to the inner being with the help of external distractions," depriving " the person of the ability to control their own energy.

Ding is the second of the two main principles of Taoist meditation. Ding is the concentration and focus of the mind and breath, which when used in conjunction with the immobility of Jing, since the state is "one-sided consciousness"; an emotional state that is not disturbed, disturbed, or disturbed. This is the goal of striving to practice Taoist meditation.

Along with these two principles, a corresponding breathing technique was achieved. Focusing on the air flow inside and outside the body, working to achieve a soft, smooth, and slow breathing technique requires a little practice. Some find it useful to focus on an object such as a flame to free their inner confidence from all other distractions. Others prefer to simply close their eyes, separating obsessive thoughts from concentration on breathing. Mantras are frequently used in Taoist meditation, was considered focused on the mind for centuries if you are using energy. There are special mantras that are effectively used: "om" - to stabilize the body;" Ah "- to suppress energy and" drone", which focuses on the mind.

Many people spend a lot of time perfecting the art of Taoist meditation, especially in these tense times of economic uncertainty, when a sense of balance and peace is so needed. While full control of the inner energy and mind requires a lot of practice and time, getting rid of the daily stress and anxiety of everyday life is worth it.

Philosophy of Taoism

What are the basic principles?

A person is usually a social being who finds meaning more often from his relationships with others and with a higher being. They say that the goal in which you do something will largely determine how you do it. It is a case of life, purpose and faith that forces him to live the quality of life that you will have. Taoism is the" path " in life, it provides the meaning of life and the principles that the believer will lead. Here is a summary of the principles that govern Taoism.

Tao:

Analysts said Tao supports principles compatible with the laws of nature. It's not far from the truth. After all, the principles of Tao describe the path of learning that every person must follow. This principle is also an attempt to answer what, in fact, is the source of the universe. This is an attempt to explain what is and what is not. This principle says that energy or QI and its direction of flow determine the state of being, and the universe, and personality. If you want peace, you must apply this principle of Taoism.

De or Te:

This principle tells how to activate the Tao principle. This emphasizes the need for humility and honesty in the use of the power of Taoism. As a lifestyle de points out that active enforcement of the Tao principle is the only way to exercise their power.

Wu Wei:

In direct translation, Wu Wei refers to " do it effortlessly. "That is, as a believer in Taoism, you do not have to force things in your own way. This differs from most principles applied in the West. With regard to these principles such as capitalism, waiting to use other, and use all your forces to achieve your goal. A Taoist who is not destined to fight for what they do on your way. Instead, we expect to move on to higher forces that will ultimately dominate human events. The ability to give up the power of the universe leads to a sense of peace.

P U":

This principle of Taoism emphasizes the need to be simple and reconciled with yourself. This principle, which results in an undiluted block, emphasizes the need to have a clean perception of events. So Taoist must take control over events miss of nature, without trying to read more than you see. In this way, the believer is always taught and receives the results of Mother Nature. So, as a believer and an intern, there is never anything good or bad, that's fine.

Taoist Spirituality and Psychotherapy

Lao Tzu and his fine works of Tao Dau Jing (or Tao Dau Jing) guided the ancient Chinese through a chaotic and tumultuous period of political, social and spiritual crisis during the period of the warring state. Lao Tzu's radical thinking and learning separated from Confucius's study of values, family organization, Good Governance and social harmony.

The Lao-Tseu study focused on the concept of Wei (leave / leave / no-Action). Wu Wei does not mean that we do not behave or do nothing, but basically teaches us not to force, control or interfere with ourselves, as well as others. Allowing and without distractions, our mind is motionless and empty, so we act or act as open, flexible and adaptive as possible.

In my work as a psychotherapist and in my personal experience, I find that this is often our greatest criticism. Our mind constantly and inexorably judges all our feelings, thoughts and behaviors. Judgments prevent us from living in the present moment and from living fully as we continue to speak in our heads of right or wrong, agreement or disagreement. So, we try to control or limit things and interfere with the natural flow of things, limiting, limiting or establishing a barrier against ourselves. Wei's idea can guide us on the path to emotional and psychological health.

I often remind my clients to be kind, not to disturb observers of our thoughts and feelings and to let everything happen. Our emotional pain and suffering intensifies when we ask a question, judge harshly and try to reject unwanted feelings. Do you have the experience of trying to stop being nervous? And the palms begin to sweat, your heart short, and your face is bright red, and you are more nervous than it should be. By allowing, without being distracted or needing changes, we can perform or act in a more natural and adaptive way.

Spirit And Taoism

Medical sciences have adopted mind meditation techniques. It reduces stress levels in patients and improves symptoms of various diseases such as depression, anxiety, blood pressure, skin infections, chronic pain and heart failure.

The complexity of the modern world has paved the way for chronic stress. Meditation has been practiced since ancient times in China and India to relieve stress problems. The writing of Taoism and Confucianism refers to the techniques of stress relief through meditation.

Chinese Roots Of Meditation Hunting

John Kabat Zinn was based on Zen Buddhism at 19. Century NL the ancient Chinese practiced sophisticated techniques to provide stress, including breathing and meditation. Historians believe that the adherents of Buddhism, Confucianism and Lao-Tsu have collected their teachings that will serve as a guiding principle for future generations. The peaceful approach allowed the force to cope with the difficulties of war, death and loss of property.

Taoism appeared during the reign of the Shang dynasty, but the official records of practice and learning did not survive. Lao Tzu began the formal writing of these teachings in Tao Da Ching, the central source of Taoism. Includes 81 separate chapters. Chang-Xie, another text of Tao was compiled in 3. and 4. century B. eu. The Chinese consider the text a social, political, spiritual and philosophical classic.

Chinese Philosophy And Medicine

In western medicine, he sees the heart as a pump of blood circulation in all parts of the body, while the brain is the thought organ for perception, memory, feelings, intuition and decision-making. Chinese philosophy does not distinguish the brain and heart. The heart is a spirit that works in tandem with a dynamic environment. The goal is to create a harmony between the blue and the environment.

Stress Relief-Confucian Approach

Confucius, a Chinese philosopher, developed this school of thought during the government struggle. He believed that the true happiness of a person depends on social harmony. Its formation is based on the principle that there is a social harmony in which people act responsibly and treat others with respect, empathy and confidence. He stressed that people should live practically according to an appropriate ethical behavior model. His teachings are designed to ensure a virtuous life with respect and loyalty.

Confucius says that social War and political instability have caused individual stress. He believed that people need to develop social harmony to lead a stress-free life. He mentioned the principles that the ruling class should apply to promote social assistance and harmony. Unfortunately, his council did not follow the ruling class, he continues to fight, which imposes problems on ordinary people.

Taoist Philosophy Of Stress Relief

Taoism has proposed triple measures to reduce chronic stress problems.

Jing-Man must be free from prejudices such as norms, values, dichotomies, differences, concepts, judgments and theories that control his behavior.

Wei has another measure: disrespect for Self-interference with others.

Shi-the third step is to avoid participating in world affairs.

Compliance with these steps requires self-improvement that involves impartial observation and participation in the current environment. Guan refers to a state of receptivity, a calm and clear observation, where he tries to understand himself, the current situation and business, rather than having an idea of reality. A person experiences Tao in his real state without affecting the attitude of others to the nature of Tao.

When you reach the status of guano, you create an unbiased view of the world that influences your thoughts, emotions, decisions and behaviors. You realize that there is no definitive or biased concept and that there are different ways to handle situations. You will realize that you have several options for assessing and managing a particular situation. You realize that you are excluded from the dynamic world by following firm principles that try to escape reality. This moment of consciousness creates harmony with the natural world, therefore an effective source of stress.

The empty blue allows you to experience the Tao for free. Robert Santi, philosopher, believes that the phenomenon acts as a source of delicate force, allowing man to act naturally according to the constantly changing needs of nature.

The importance of breathing

The tenth verse for Tae Jing says that we must breathe as a child naturally and uncompromisingly. We need to focus on our breathing and let go of anxious thoughts and emotions. It is necessary to monitor the process of free and simple breathing. Breathing is the main activity of any living being. We breathe for the first time at birth and die with the last breath. Breathing in harmony with nature allows freedom. Limited breathing causes fatigue and tension because Xin experiences a closed, inflexible, harsh, frightening and hostile nature. This creates stress and paves the way for a brutal breathing cycle.

In the sixth chapter of Chuang Tzu, there was a difference between deep breathing (from the heel) and superficial breathing (from the neck). Shallow breathing is a symptom of confusion, limitation, stress and negative thoughts, while deep breathing refers to calmness, clarity and conscious blue. The child experiences free breathing because he is not affected by tension and other restrictions. In contrast, adults do not have the freedom to breathe.

Space and its advantages

Deep breathing relaxes and the body of restrictive thoughts, judgments and values. It cleans the inner self and balances the energy, allowing them to move freely. Lama Tartang Tulku thinks that this feeling is stronger than the expression of joy-it's huge, deep and infinite.

Practice Qigong and Buddhist Spirit

The practice of Buddhist consciousness is aimed at disappearance or Anichka. There is a deep connection between the concept of Anik and Qi, a Taoist concept. Mindfulness focuses on mental images, physical feelings, inner speech and emotional feelings of the body; this makes ordinary experiences unusual. Feelings and thoughts flow like an energy that expands, pulsates, pulls and vibrates. In turn, Qigong, the practice of internal alchemy involves exercises to create this experience with the flow of energy. The combination of these two practices combines the best of both worlds. Mindfulness routines strengthen attention, the ability to decipher light energy in an ordinary experience. Qigong delicately activates the living energy. Chinese Medicine combines hunting as a fluid energy flow through different parts of the body. The disease is caused when pulsatile energy is not enough in the human body.

The practice of Qigong combines these imbalances to eliminate stagnation and create harmony between the flow of energy and the Xin. Ingenuity helps us to openly accept the internal experiences of mind and body, completing the procedures of Qigong. The combination increases potency for deep healing.

Taoism and Stress

In Taoism, we often talk about life that has a "flow" or behaves "like water".""We will achieve this by avoiding and overcoming obstacles and limitations. We do this by relaxing: "we slowly accept things," looking for the flow of the world and going with it. People I've spoken to over the years have asked me what makes laziness different from laziness to stay here and say we all do it. This is a big difference!

Laziness, when a person takes responsibility for what he is responsible for, what needs to be done, or even what he wants to do. This behavior can lead to even more suffering and stress. Laziness literally resists the flow of the world, which is ugly, as if you are doing something wrong all over the world. Relaxation and laziness are two completely different things.

Relax or "float downstream", in the Taoist sense, when we lose our fears and fears and we are just in the moment. You can be completely relaxed at home, at work, even in a key situation. This is a very important concept. The key doesn't necessarily slow down, because you can't always do it in a key situation. We are trying to do our best and understand that this is what we are doing now and here.

If you take an injured friend to the emergency room, you obviously can't afford to switch off or slow it down. Your duty is to help your friend, and that's why you need to relax in this flow. Fear of driving can lead to a car accident, or worse. It is much more important to stay active and at this point be ready to do everything possible to bring your friend to the hospital.

I mean, there's a way to relax in any situation. Exercises that can help you in considering when you are. When you start to feel that stress is attacking your flow, when you feel that tension in your shoulder blades, shrinking in temples, think about it.

Why is it so stressful?

It's up to you, but what do you want to do?

Why did he hit you so hard?

Are you sure you're reacting like this?

Can you let it go?

Try to do this the next time you start doing something. Relaxing under pressure, really at the right time, is a skill, which means you can learn and develop it. in fact, you can already have it on one level or another. Find out where your milestone is, where your stress starts to affect you and starts from there.

What Is a Taoist Diet?

To truly understand the Taoist regime, you must first understand a little Taoist beliefs. Taoism takes place in the heart of East Asia and Chinese cultures and has deep roots in the 2000s, although it only spread to the West in more modern times, when people begin to reject materialism for deeper spiritual understanding.

Taoists are humble egos that emphasize compassion, humility and moderation, while others are emphasized by their minimalist eating habits.

Although Taoism is not known, however, breaks the rules for his opinions inactive care, focuses on the human connection with nature and, therefore, does not believe in the hard way and ordered of modern society, deciding to follow the natural flow of the universe. The general Taoist term Yin and Yang refers to the positive and negative energies of the universe.

Five colors blind eyes.

Five tones muffle the hearing.

Five flavors confuse languages.

Fast horses and exciting hunting make the wild and crazy spirits.

Rare and expensive things make people on the street.

That's why Sage weighs the stomach, not the eye,

he always ignores it and chooses it.

I Gave You Chings, Part 12.

Historically, the Taoist diet consisted mainly of fresh fruits and vegetables, with little meat and no cereals-as they thought, during the process of digestion, creatures like the demon would be freed from the rot of cereals and would try to eat them from the inside. In the most modern times, the diet changed and began to be based mainly on the consumption of whole grains and fresh fruits and vegetables according to tradition.

The Taoist diet connects the five main flavors with the element of nature: sweet (earthy), salty (water), acidic (wood), bitter (fire), spicy (metal). They believe that greed and the rise of one taste on one pedestal on another make you feel the taste, so it is important to balance the flavors to achieve inner harmony.

Taoism is all natural and people are part of nature. One of the beliefs most important is "eat food alone", that is, to avoid artificial substances, artificial that the body can not metabolize, and they can contain the flavors unbalanced, like artificial additives, medicines, etc., - highly processed foods that contain little or does not have nutritional value, like white flour, sugar, this is not something that the body should consume and do not grow from the ground, so they are not actually a "food" suitable natural to the body human consumption.

Historically

Most of the classical Taoist literature speaks a lot about the sages of antiquity-or people who existed in prehistoric times. Some texts suggest that they exist only when they breathe and do not consume food at all. They lived as born and received food only from the Qi or Yin-Yang of the universe.

This practice, known as "Bigoo", is sometimes used as part of some Taoist traditions and mythological ideas, but it is not something that is practical or even safe for modern people living in a normal society to try. Taoists believe that man has changed, and since then the Old State has decreased, which means that it is perfectly acceptable to eat food.

It is believed that the early Taoists had a regime that reflected this vision of wise and enlightened masters even before History and before Agricultural Development. Therefore, in the early traditions, the Taoists did not eat cereals.

There can be several reasons for this-from health problems, to compliance with some mythological, agricultural factors of the past and even other social factors. The minimalist approach is often used to explain this, arguing that the Taoists do not live only from food and unconsciously receive energy from space.

However, as mentioned above, the reason he refuses to eat cereal in many of the first texts is that it does not excite the "three verses".

3 verses

A first mythological explanation of wheat abstinence is 3 verses.

These are literally 3 demonic worms that live in the human intestine and are responsible for the disintegration of the body after death.

Of course, since their goal is to devour your body, it is in their interest to die as quickly as possible.

Until death, these three worms will live in the human intestine by eating a rotten biological substance that is digested.

So, when your intestines digested the grain, 3 worms ate the waste that was produced. When they fed on cereals, they became stronger and later they could feed on the rest of your body, making you die faster.

Since the longevity of continuing to grow is one of the main goals of many Taoist practices, the purpose of the diet was to "starve" 3 verses by reducing the consumption of cereals or completely excluding it.

From a modern point of view, it is possible that the early Taoists just noticed a correlation between caloric intake and aging or poor health.

Assuming that a cell has a finite number of possible divisions during the entire life cycle, it would be necessary to significantly slow the metabolic process to slow down the process of cell division.

Another possibility mentioned earlier is simply a tribute to a docile and docile period when people were not engaged in agriculture and did not participate in social activities and games of excessive food production.

Third immortal, the King says to the King::

"Reach the Tao avoiding all the grains. You will never have to keep up with the rhythm of the Moon and the plant or crop.

In this way, people of mysterious antiquity reached old age because they remained at a minimum and never ate cereals."

As Dai Zhang says (verse of the Great existence) ::

Of the five seeds, a chisel that shortens life.,

Feel five organs and cut our holes.

One day he got into our stomach,

We no longer have the chance to live long enough.

The goal is to completely avoid all deaths

Keep the intestines without discharge!"

While many ancient Taoists practiced abstinence from cereals, this is not entirely true. There is a lot of evidence that the Taoists ate or literally searched for rice.

Perhaps abstinence from cereals was more a purification process or a kind of fasting that led to important rituals, ceremonies or rituals, such as taking long-term medications, fasting, taking elixirs and so on.

Mode

Recently, the typical diet has radically changed to focus primarily on the cereal-based diet rather than practicing complete abstinence from cereals. Even if there are radical people who claim to never eat, they are often ridiculed by the media and then discover that they are" hungry " for attention, not real old-fashioned Taoists.

The modern Taoist diet mainly adheres to the basic theory of Yin-Yang and 5 elements and relies heavily on unprocessed whole grains, fresh vegetables (especially root vegetables) and very little meat.

It is important that the vegetables are eaten at the exact time of the year and are steamed or fried. The kitchen takes natural goodness. Fruits usually dried or cooked, and the consumption of tropical fruit is incompatible considered unbalanced five fragrances because of its strong, often citrus flavor. It is also important seasonal and without any human intervention.

As a rule, all red and blue meat, including pork, rabbit, snails and others, should be avoided. Bird and game can be eaten as well as fish. However, Fish and other seafood should be consumed only once a week because of the large amount of Yin. Some fish, such as salmon, shark, swordfish and mackerel, which are very Yin, should be avoided completely.

Drinking alcohol, caffeine and chewing / smoking tobacco is intended for their refined nature.

The modern Taoist relies on moderation in his eating habits and should try to avoid eating something too much (garlic, ginger, onion, etc.).)

Differences Between The Taoist Regime And The Modern Western Regime

In the West, lifestyle and eating habits contributed to a sharp increase in such problems as heart disease, obesity, stress, cancer, arthritis and so on.

Attention has shifted from initial Prevention (a natural, healthy diet) to medication and surgery. However, an ounce of prevention is worth a pound of treatment. Why try to fight the disease, when it is rooted, when, with some simple guidelines, we can avoid it in the first place?

The modern Taoist regime, in contrast to the modern Western regime, is:

Quick overview

high energy

Enriched with vitamins and minerals

Easy digestibility for the body

Raw and processed

This means that daily Western foods such as bread and milk, which we believe are perfectly healthy, are considered almost poisonous to strict Taoists. Instead, rice and soy milk are used as substitutes, and skim milk is usually taken.

The "Salt Up" Approach"""

Qigong: refers to a set of Taoist exercises used to maintain and move with Chi (the energy of the Universe). Methods include meditation and focusing on physical movements. This helps maintain physical and mental health.

As a rule, in many types of Taoist qigong, energy is taken from the earth. Similarly, the term "carrot" is at the heart of Taijiquan and many Chinese martial arts and Taoism, so historically and in a Taoist context, the country's authorities were considered the best way to get vital energy from food.

Like Taoist qigong, the Taoist diet emphasizes the "salt" approach to vegetable consumption. This means that the plant should be consumed in a large percentage of the total diet, especially in underground (root vegetables), compared to a higher one, such as an Apple.

The main reason for this was that ground vegetables have more energy and the ability to supply the body with more Chi. It is believed that potatoes, all kinds of root crops, potatoes, carrots, beets, to name a few, provide good energy to the soil, which helps the spleen (immune system) become stronger, and Jing Qi more "roots".

After all, the plants attached to the Ground were as green as cabbage, Chinese cabbage, spinach, and so on, which were often pickled or stored for the winter.

Then came the highest crops: peppers, tomatoes, eggplants, etc., which were used to provide good energy, but on a smaller scale.

Zao Wou-Ki, Creativity and Taoism Thought

Zao Wou-Ki, the deceased Chinese-French painter joined the art of calligraphy with impressionism by merging eastern and western art. I recently read his obituary and it made me think about the artistic process and creativity. I wanted to use his life as a starting point for exploring the art and Taoist thinking, in particular, therefore, that his second wife suffered from deep depression and committed suicide.

These different themes intersect in Za's life. As a child, he learned the art of calligraphy is strongly influenced by Taoist philosophy, and when he arrived in Paris in 1948 (before the communist revolution), went with his wife to Paris, where he settled in the same block, in the district of Montparnasse, where Othon communism-a well-known painter in the Fauvist movement was the organization of the dao of movement.

The tragedy of the depression falls on his life, when his wife Chu Ching, the star of the Chinese cinema the great beauty became a critically acclaimed sculptor, who committed suicide at the peak of its success. This must have had a significant impact on the emotional content of his paintings

Zao's work was similar in style to the abstract impressionist painters who significantly influenced his thoughts, when he visited New York City and said that Matisse, Cezanne and Picasso were also very influential in their style. Interestingly, when reading his style of painting, there is a big emphasis on western influences, but little on its Chinese roots, in particular the Taoist thinking. In China calligraphy generally focuses on the proper design of Chinese characters and the ability to do so was an essential element of chinese culture, as well as Taoist thinking, so it is impossible to completely separate the writing from the basic elements of Taoism.

One of the main elements of Taoist thinking in relation to Chinese calligraphy and French

Impressionists is the role of intuition. This addresses Chuang TSU's great Taoist essay, which told the story of the demonstration of the connection between creativity and intuition, he said and paraphrased.

Once a carpenter on a bicycle for a trolley in the courtyard of the palace fence. When he looked up, he noticed a strong Duke reading in a nearby room. He laid his instruments, came to the Duke and asked. May I ask What Your Royal Highness reads? The duke replied: "I have read the works of great lords and sages. The Carpenter asked: "Do the wise LIVE?"No," the duke replied, " They died a long time ago."The carpenter, who asked even more, asked the Duke if they were dead, so the words you read are just sequins left by the Ancients. The Duke became increasingly angry, looked firmly at the carpenter and replied: "I read and got angry. What does the bicycle manufacturer know about books or knowledge? Your questions are offensive. You better explain it to me. If you can defend your point of view, I'll let you go, and if you can't, I'll have you killed.'

"Without fear," Carpenter replied. Let me tell you something about Carpenter's work. If I make the Rays too tight, they don't fit the wheel, and if I release them, the wheel falls off. I have to adapt to perfection. I have power in my hands and I judge my intuition. In the process there is an element that can not be described in words. I can not teach my child this intuitive element, nor teach him himself. Here I am at the age of seventy years, living master of the art manufacturing bicycles. the old masters died a long time ago and that something could not describe the communication died with them. That's Why Your Majesty reads the drunkenness of an old man.'

Now Zao has died, and like the former master of his art, he can be considered a bullet that escapes the ancients. He took his genius with him, but we can experience the Masterpiece grass on the canvas.

Lewis Harrison is pioneering author, speaker and practical philosopher specializing in human potential and personal development.

Lewis runs Life coaching and two residential shelters at the Harrison Center for personal development in Stamford NY.

Chinese Philosophies Amidst Political Turmoil

In response to the political turmoil associated with the warring States period in China (403-221 p.No, email.) there were different schools of thought. Among them are Confucianism, Taoism and the arrival of the silk road, and Buddhism. One can understand and resist the two root philosophies and recognize the reasons why Confucianism was finally approved by the government and not by Taoism, although both may not be practiced exclusively. Understanding this, one can understand why Mahayana Buddhism in the form of Chan began to compete with Confucianism around the 19th century, P.

Confucianism was conceived and named after Kong Fuza (551-479 BC), known as the philosopher Kong, to his disciples and Confucius in the West. Like his contemporary, the Buddha Siddarta Guatama did not deal with metaphysical problems. His rationale was that guesses about these issues have nothing to do with the ethical, moral, or political scene, but are therefore useless. He believed that the right balance of these three important topics would seem easy by improving individual human relations, and would even reject public Affairs as symptoms of this basic disease: inadequate human relations. Educating people and turning them into Jun or higher persons would help progress in the development of human relations. These people would be official in an ideal government. As the Chinese adopted the philosophy of merging the Congo as a substitute for legalism, the government even encouraged its education system in an attempt to produce junze.

Taoism emphasizes the reconciliation of our human consciousness with the nature of everything, or the Tao. Taoism was attributed to a person known as Lao Tzu, and although the purportedly written text, the Tao-da Ching (classics on the road and virtue) was also known as Lao Tzu, so it is currently impossible to determine whether Lao Tzu exists. Most likely, there were 4 different hands. century B. had. despite the fact that Lao Tzu, the modern Kong

Fuzi is said to live in the 19th century. Lao Tzu, whose name can be translated as "old teacher", was considered archived in one of the small kingdoms. In Taoist practice, this can be realized by the idea of Wei Wu-Wei, or by an action without actions that can be understood as if it were done without understanding. Once this is done, one agrees with the Tao. This idea is very similar to Congo Fuzi's idea that the characters will automatically restore their human relationships and come into harmony with the basic virtue of Rene's humanity. When asked to explain this idea, Kong Fuzi refused because, like Tao, the Ren that can be described is not the real REN. Unclear. The emphasis on Taoism is more mystical, while Confucianism focuses on ethical and political applications. Neither of them excludes the other, and they are both known to practice government officials in the evening after performing their duties in the workplace.

These two philosophies served to harmonize individuals and society in a certain way. Taoism is really an individual experience, and by definition it cannot be shared with others. If all people understood the Tao, people would become Autonomous, and the problems of the day would collapse as stupidity. This idea is utopian, it is theoretically beautiful, but not practical, and for this, that Confucianism was adopted by the Chinese government, as it deals with issues of more land-based ethics and politics, but with the same basic ideas that are labeled differently. This seemed more relevant to the average person and their problems. In the end, he found an opponent in Buddhism.

Buddhism has an idea similar to Jun, called a Buddha or Bodhisattva. The equivalent of a Confucian troglodyte will be cultivated based on the practice of the noble eight. This path leads to wisdom and compassion, which are synonymous with virtue. This aspect of Buddhism is very similar to Confucianism, and the prospect of the end of suffering in the Four Noble Truths would be very attractive to professionals of this kind of philosophy who did not pay attention to such thoughts. Due to the lack of emphasis on political Affairs and subsequent entry into China was Buddhism, the government never sanctioned as much as Confucianism.

These three forms in question arose or were adopted due to the political chaos of the warring States in the 18th and 4th centuries. in China. Each philosophy is very similar, but has its own special differences that are subject to different applications in the enterprise. All survive to this day.

Taoism For Leader

There are two points of view that determine the quality of leadership. Internal factors include character traits and resulting behaviors; external factors include leadership and follower context. Researchers of Behavioral Research believe that internal factors of character, personality and behavior affect external factors. However, another school believes that external factors affect the leadership process. Modern scientists emphasize the importance of internal factors of leaders and followers: their knowledge, cognition and experience affect leadership.

New theories about leadership try to suggest that factors of intrinsic character with their resulting behavior significantly affect the essence of leadership. Relative leadership theories emphasize the importance of external and internal factors for effective leadership. Interaction between leaders and their supporters plays an important role in determining the quality of leadership. Skeptics criticize all theories about leadership on the basis of insufficient evidence and questionable leadership techniques.

Taoism generates awareness of the universe, of humanity and its connection with nature. Philosophy emphasizes that any universal phenomenon consists of interdependent factors, but at the same time competing in nature. Taoists believe that leadership is a process that exists in human society and is based on human relations with the masses. So, you cannot ignore the basics of Taoism, which need a balanced, constantly changing and interdependent relationship between two contradicting inner forces.

A careful analysis of different theories about leadership suggests that leadership styles are based on the principles of Taoism. The Taoist leadership position believes that leaders and followers share interchangeable relationships, not because leaders follow their leaders and obey as followers, the situation could change over time. External factors are competitive in a single system of leadership or dictatorship. In small leadership systems, internal and external forces work together.

Scientists distinguish two Yang-Yin systems: context and leadership contribute to the relationship between environmental factors and organizational factors. Another system, which includes followers and leaders, develops a smaller Yang-Yin system. Taoism considers the context and the guidelines should be the same some parts of the leadership system as related issues that have a broader context are related to a broader leadership style. Regardless of the severity of the context, there are final problems that affect a certain leadership.

Taoism sees human society as a smaller system than the Yang-Yin universe. Each person represents the Yang and yin microsystem. Taoism States: "humanity follows the rules of the Earth, which in turn follow the rules of heaven (or the universe). The sky (or the universe) follows the rules of the Tao and the Tao follows its nature " (Xiong, 2005)."

The process of Yang and Yin does not repeat itself, but occurs in an ascending or descending cycle. Leaders and followers can take Yang and Yin positions at different stages of the development cycle. Every object in the universe undergoes eternal change. Leadership research begins the study of individual traits and goes back to new theories based on transformative, visionary and charismatic changes in personality.

Taoism considers dynamic leadership by nature. This allows leaders and followers to exercise dominance of power. The balance in the strength of the two entities is short-lived. Yang is a dynamic and active force, while Yin is a calm and passive force. Leaders are seen as yang when they show power proactively and progressively, while disciples act as Yin when they are less active and passive. Otherwise, leaders are Yin when they do not actively participate, and followers are yang when they actively participate in growth and success. Leadership is determined by the dominant strength of the organization. The nature of leadership determines which power currently dominates the organization. So, we will consider this point in more detail when we look at successful models of leader traits based on Taoism.

Success Stories of Taoist Leadership

To understand dynamic leadership, a model of the fundamental traits of a successful leader based on Taoist principles was created. The model reflects dynamic leadership, as well as the leadership theories that have managed to follow this model. This model assumes that there are five main traits for developing a successful leader.

Successful leaders at the child stage of the organization must have the characteristics of Yan, that is, initiatives and progressive. At this stage, the leader must win the support and faith of his supporters, who, in turn, must understand the mission and vision of the organization. The child's installation requires the participation of all its members, the leader must show care, love, care and, most importantly, listen to his followers. It solves the small mistakes of its followers by encouraging them to be creative and increase innovation. Since it requires everyone to contribute, it is not strict and collects advice from followers. He consciously supports good talents, taking care of their desires and needs to achieve personal success. Leadership achieves rapid growth for its organization by leveraging the innovative and creative abilities of its followers. He is praised for his charisma and recognition of his success.

The second stage of the organization's growth is associated with rapid development, which the leader sees in a fiery position. The organization is entering a strong phase of the Jan. Managers are energetic and enthusiastic about the success of the organization and are active at every step. They are implementing new strategies to increase the bandwidth of their subscribers to increase the growth and revenue of a successful organization. Any successful business venture is the result of the continuing progressive efforts of its leader.

Taoism, however, believes that the leader should display the qualities of accuracy in the second stage. The leader is in a strong position in relation to his supporters. The rapid success of an organization can overwhelm leaders, thereby encouraging them to practice some unrealistic programs that followers can't object to. At the moment, many companies have failed because of unrealistic goals. Thus, the leader must achieve realistic goals with precision, enthusiasm, and encouragement.

The third stage sees the leaders in the position of the earth, the stage of maturity institution. Leaders have a stable growth perspective, and a balance between supporters and leadership is being established. Harmony reaches its ideal state by enjoying stable and effective communication relationships. Taoism believes that the leader at this stage demonstrates loyalty and loyalty. A leader is an honest person who is true to his responsibility and maintains transparency with his followers. He adopts a democratic leadership style in which followers can easily predict his behavioral line. Understanding the leader and his supporters is the most important factor in the success of an organization.

However, at this stage, different approaches can be applied to achieve success. Despite the balance, the leader can choose to convince the follower to accept his views. In addition, the leader can become more democratic, give value to followers, and exchange opinions, motivating their contributions. Some leaders may allow followers to provide their best efforts. This allows you to listen to advice provided by followers. At the moment, the leader acts as an intermediary in relation to the driving force of the Organization.

The fourth stage of the organization's development puts the leader in the position of metal. The company is experiencing its maturity and is beginning to decline. The organization is governed by a rigid structure, and organizational functions are not active. The leader adopts a conservative leadership style that scares creative followers. Some smart followers are enjoying this situation and exploring their own business. To succeed at this stage, a leader needs characteristic of managerial skills, fairness, regulation, and adequate power to motivate followers and improve their contribution. It requires responsibility, capable of rewarding followers and berating the selfish followers.

The last stage of leadership is the water stage, in which the organization reaches the dying stage. The organization loses the support of its creative followers, and the company reaches the transition between birth and death. A wise leader, currently working well. This creates an encouraging prospect of solving current problems, convincing it followers to solve problems and promise a bright future. Create a new vision for creating a new organization to win the trust of the faithful. It presents visionary skills to encourage capable followers.

However, Taoist principles only act as a basis for classifying fundamental theories of leadership. Since there are many factors that are currently being developed a leadership model, we need countless theories to understand the characteristics of a true leader. Taoism claims that leadership styles are dynamic due to constantly changing external and internal factors. A theory can explain events that fit a particular pattern; however, the cycle undergoes continuous changes, so several theories take time. There is no definitive theory that can accurately classify different leadership styles.

Researchers now isolate the factors of leadership to the changing contexts, drawing conclusions from an isolated point of view. Because they do not take into account external and internal contexts, leadership theories are not relevant to real events. Despite their limitations, modern leadership theories should not be dismissed as garbage. Modern theories are an integration of the principles of all leadership theories.

This requires that leaders demonstrate appropriate traits in accordance with changing situations. Leadership develops in Yang in some cases of leadership and Yin in other stages. Hey, he should change his behavior accordingly. For example, in water and on land, the leader must show the behavior of an observer. It should accept changes in the organizational structure, and not follow the same behavior that is practiced in the early stages. The Taoist principle effectively describes real events, so the boss comes to a reasonable decision.

The Tao te Ching verse offers an effective working principle for successful leaders. He says: "If you want to be a great leader, you need to learn to follow the Tao.

A leader who follows Taoist principles should abandon strict strategies and concepts and define. Instead of following a complex concept, the leader follows his natural instincts, and his actions are governed by the principles of nature. This time, it may be absurd for a person who retreats into strategic leadership. Taoist principles believe that planning is not as effective as it allows businesses to operate independently. This will be a term for understanding this rare type of leadership, since this method is no better than strategic planning.

Do not limit

The Taoist leader allows his supporters to function without any restrictions. The ban of any kind removes the virtues and creativity of followers. This can lead to aggressive outbursts of followers, and a sense of insecurity enters the mind of followers.

Confidence

Taoism believes that the leader must be autonomous. Followers must feel safe, which means that they need everything they need to maintain their existence. Followers must be motivated to take responsibility for their activities and not to be constantly monitored. This is in conflict with a radical approach that leaders trying to control your subordinates, place to force them to grow on their own. Followers must have the skills to be less dependent on their superiors.

Prohibition Of Law

Tao Te Jing says that in the absence of strict rules, laws and regulations, supporters adopt an honest work ethic. He believes abandoning Economic Planning will make people richer. Freedom of will and control is better than leadership, which exercises control through policies, plans, retaliatory measures and rules. But a Leader who does not voluntarily exercise control guarantees better control in an organization that believes in self-government. This allows the principles of Tao to rule the people. The leader must trust the abilities of DAO. order can be maintained even without strategic and political plans. The Leader must give up spending on strategic planning and policy development.

An important question was whether these tools are constructive or harmful to the organization. Modern business leaders develop short-term policies and strategic plans due to market dynamics and geopolitics. The overall benefit can naturally come from the ever-changing dynamics that leaders need to consider.

Taoism believes that the leader simply does not interfere in the affairs of the world and encourages others to follow his example. The goal of obtaining a common advantage allows the leader to apply the principles of Taoism in his organization.

Wei Wu Wei

Taoism explains the general principles for solving the concept of modern leadership. Taoist philosophers determined the basic characteristics of the leader and explained the strategic directions for many human activities. Activities range from the management of state affairs, with the culture of virtues and morals of people. Thus, understanding the Taoist principles of leadership is excellent information. The Taoists believe that the leaders are no different from the disciples. A person who most serves his people is considered a leader. The principle of Wei wu Wei emphasized spontaneous leadership in a natural way. Respects the natural course of events, without any interference. The holistic view of the Tao allows individuals to consider themselves as part of the universe, thereby cooperating with the natural rhythm of life.

Wei Wu Wei consists of three principles of leadership management. The first principle is " do something without doing something else. "The second principle allows the natural flow of events with non-interference. The third principle concerns symbolic leadership. 10097 words

Chapter 60 Tao Te Ching States: "the leadership of a large organization or state is like cooking small fish."As well as excessive mixing adversely affects the preparation of small fish, excessive interference of imbalance in the workplace. To cultivate the principles of the Tao, the leader must allow natural events to create challenges and naturally explore solutions. The natural flow allows the Tao to harmonize with all things or individuals. The practice of positive inactivity, that is, Wei Wu Wei, allows events to monitor its natural course to respect universal forces. Leaders must adhere to the basic principles and adapt to the constantly changing dynamics of nature. Leaders must agree between non-interference the natural flow of events and efforts to change the natural flow.

There are four types of leadership qualities. The Leader strategically manages his supporters and allows them to work independently, without interrupting their activities. In addition, the leader is human, that is, cares about the needs of his disciples. Another type of leader carries out punishment and control through policies, rules and regulations. The fourth type of leader does not believe in Taoist principles, and his supporters despise him. The best form of leadership is the first type, which is based on the Wei Wu Wei ideology of Taoism.

Western Management Theory Vs. Taoism

Douglas McGregor has developed leading theories, namely Theory X and theory Y. Theory X believes in a leadership style that applies compliance and control. Leaders take different situations, such as: followers avoid work, how they do not like, they do not feel that they need to be guided; they are ready to accept responsibility, and therefore demand supervision to achieve organizational goals. The theory promotes a leadership style focused on people management through engagement, delegation and cooperation. This theory believes that followers are eager to take their responsibilities; they are ready to work and take initiatives to achieve the goals of the organization. Followers help their leaders achieve their goals through positive reinforcement.

McGregor developed another theory, known as theory Y. This highlights management or leadership through contribution, cooperation and delegation. According to Theory Y, people want to work, are willing to accept responsibility, and are ambitious and show initiative to achieve the goal. People can achieve goals with positive motivation.

Abraham Maslow promoted the theory of hierarchical needs. It is largely influenced by Taoist principles and emphasizes self-realization and human dignity. Maslow believes that any style of individual leadership affects only a few cases. The Taoist leader is far from having the power to teach his disciples. A direct link between Taoism and human psychology can be found through the concept of leadership developed by Maslow.

But there are some consequences of the Taoist leadership.

First, modern researchers are less aware of Maslow's theory of leadership. Taoism offers a broad perspective for academic, social and behavioral purposes. Secondly, Taoism helps modern leaders practice effective leadership. Taoism can fill the void in the Western philosophy of people management. Third, research studies based on Taoist leadership emphasize the empirical examination of social, behavioral and Management Sciences. In addition, studies on Taoism reduce human conflicts. Taoist principles create harmony of themselves with nature and other living beings. Today's world resembles a global Village, and residents are engaged in many human and ecological interests. Perhaps Taoism is the most valuable asset for the world's population.

Taoist Tai Chi For a Change, Getting Real Peace

Taoist tai chi is a soft martial art (in China it is called internal art) that guarantees the well-being and health of people of all colors.

Millions of people, both Asian and other, enjoy the health benefits of the Taoist practice of Tai Chi. It is estimated that there are more than 500 specialized schools for the preparation of sand for this particular style, located in twenty-five countries around the world. Although it has existed for hundreds of years in China and Japan, the Taoist Tai Chi is the 1970s.years brought to North America by master Mo Lin-Shin.

The main goal of the Taoist is to strengthen and restore health. It is one of the mildest forms of Taiji and is ideal for the elderly and for those who regain strength for exercise. The movements are slow, thoughtful and graceful and their design should help the student develop strength and flexibility.

The practice of Taoist also helps with joint and muscle pain, as it emphasizes twists and subtle strokes. It is also useful for increasing muscle strength and improving blood circulation in the body. It also helps people who tremble or dizzy to restore a sense of balance.

The exercises are also intended to help you relieve stress and anxiety through delicate activities. It is sometimes called "Meditation in motion" because the continuity of movement combined with a sense of attention helps to heal and rejuvenate the mind and body. Since this practice is based on meditation and learning simultaneously, Taoist tai chi is also known as regenerating form of delicate exercises.

The physical component of the Taoist Taiji consists of basic principles known as "fundamentals". The whole set of bases consists of one hundred and eight movements. Some of these movements mimic the positions of the army or animals found in nature, which is typical of all species of Taiji. However, these movements are not necessarily as aggressive as very old frame styles like Chen Tai Chi style.

The general spiritual intention of the Taoist is to develop an inner sense of peace, wisdom and knowledge that puts a person in a spiritually powerful position to spread compassion and generosity to others. The goal of this is to lose all ego and egocentrism through the practice of this ancient art of" meditation in motion"."

Taoist tai chi can be somewhat compared to Alexander's technique, which focuses on relaxation, breathing, balance, posture, spine alignment, angle correction, weight transfer tracking, spiral rotations, limb detection and closure, tail bone centering, and spine stretching and alignment. Movements are soft and circular; they are performed with a concentrated but relaxed state of mind.

A key aspect of the Taoist is the acceptance of the spirit of dedication, kindness and elimination of selfishness. Taoist tai chi is not only practiced, but lives, your life can change...Perhaps constant changes will not happen overnight, and it is better to know them by their own example, showing a life in harmony, compassion and service to others.

Taoist Meditations For Healing

Taoists in China have, for thousands of years, used acupuncture, herbs, exercise, and meditation to promote health and prolong life. The techniques they have honed over the centuries are, perhaps surprisingly, perfectly suited to our modern health problems.

Taoist meditation is also easy to do for many modern people, because it engages the mind more than other meditation styles, such as watching the breath.

Taoists mainly use meditation as a spiritual practice to become one with the Tao. However, noting the health benefits of meditation, they developed techniques specifically to improve health. Health and longevity have always been important to the Taoists for two reasons. First they needed time and energy to focus on their spiritual practices. The second reason is that some sects believed in physical immortality, so they were looking for ways to extend their lives, indefinitely.

Most Taoist healing meditations make use of the energy theory of acupuncture. Skilled meditators can manipulate IQ, or vital energy, as effectively as an acupuncturist can. In addition to the flow of qi in the meridians, the Taoists have a chakra system, very similar to the Indian one, as well as a five-element system.

The five elements are energy categories. All nature is divided into one of the five elements. Each organ and tissue in your body is also divided into five elements. For example, the wooden element is associated with the liver, gallbladder, tendons and ligaments and eyes. Psychologically, it is associated with planning and organization, flexibility, anger and frustration. It is the system most vulnerable to stress. Externally, it is related to the spring season, wind and green color.

Taoist meditation can include movement, sound and / or display of colored light to clean and heal each of the five elements. If you have a problem-related wood element, you can breathe fresh green light into the area, and imagine toxic energy coming out like smoke with your breath out. Where ever the problem is, it is useful to start breathing the green light into the liver, until it is glowing green.

In Taoism there are three main chakras or energy centers in the body. One just below the navel, one in the center of the chest and one between the eyes. A simple visualization of healing is to become aware of the problem in your body. Give it a shape and color. So, imagine moving it to the nearest Energy Center, and then out of your body. Let it soar a few inches from your from the Energy Center. Then, as you exhale, imagine the white light blowing through that object. With each breath the object fades, until it disappears completely.

Can Taoist Meditation Really Bring Me Peace?

Taoist meditation, as Bruce Kumar Francis teaches, offers a way to give everyone lasting peace and a strong sense of belonging to the world. But the type of meditation system is very different from the one that most people are used to.

We use what Bruce calls the Taoist method of water. Many meditation techniques can be classified as "fire Techniques". "This means that these systems tend to cause or "burn" the negative mental and emotional effects of everyday life on this material.

On the other hand, the "water method" allows these effects to wear out gently like "water ice and carbonated water". Just as the flow gradually and gently separates the heaviest substances, this method can eliminate all the collected shit in your body, mind and mind.

This amazing system begins with a set of moving qigong called dragon & Tiger Qigong and the silence inherent in the "long-term breathing" method. Both deep systems are designed to start more advanced practices in the Taoist water method.

In addition, the practice of the short form of the Wu Tai Chi-Chuan family system (Taijiquan) and the single and double Palm will change with the Taoist art of change, Ba Gua Chang (Baguazhan) will be studied to bring the student to a higher level of integration with the universe.

So, I cannot answer the question of whether Taoist meditation can bring you peace. Everything is in you. I can tell you that the Taoist method of water will give you the tools to get there.

Ancient Taoist Secret of Lasting Longer in Bed

Taoism has developed various exercises to develop and improve its sexual strength. A technique passed down from generation to generation is called "deer exercise". In fact, it is a simple exercise for rubbing and anal contraction with such advantages as:

1. Strengthens the tissues of the genitals

2. It improves blood circulation and transports nutrients from sperm to the rest of the body

3. Replenishes energy in any weakened gland

4. Build sexual stamina

So how do you do this exercise? You will need to perform this exercise in the morning after waking up and in the evening, just before bedtime. This can be done standing, sitting or even lying down.

To perform the deer exercise, vigorously rub your hands to get warmth and energy from your body. Now quickly take your right hand and gently close your testicles(it works best when you are not wearing anything). Now place your left hand on your belly (which is two inches below your navel) and rub it at a relaxed and pleasant pace counterclockwise 81 times.

When you are done, vigorously rub your hands again and start again, the difference this time is that you change the position of the hands (the left hand destroys the testicles and the right abdomen Clockwise).

The Taoists are very focused on the use of mental concentration in their exercises. So it is not surprising that mental concentration is also part of the exercise. According to the Taoists, focusing your mind at some point on you will effectively bring IQ to this point.

Therefore, when rubbing, you need to pay all your attention to physical movements and increasing heat. Then, when your hand touches the testicles and abdomen, feel the Qi move from the hand to the testicles and abdomen.

Deer exercise is designed to be effective if you practice it every day morning and evening. However, if you want to see instant results, you can try taking herbal supplements. Herbal supplements are the safest and most effective way to last more than 20 minutes and have an effect that lasts for several days. This makes it the most popular and economical method of staying firm and lasting for a long time.

The Extraordinary Taoist Water Method

The Taoist water method, as I learned from Bruce Kumar Francis, gives every person who practices it with great honesty and humility the opportunity to integrate body, mind, and spirit into the body of the entire cosmos.

This system usually begins with an honest student learning a gentle but deep method of breathing known to some as "longevity breathing". As the name suggests, it is designed to extend the number of its years, providing a quality of life that is little present in those who are old.

From here, the next step is an often surprising set of medical qigong, commonly referred to as "Dragon and Tiger qigong". This short group of exercises without influence is often taught to cancer patients in China.

In my school, I teach the famous eight brocades of qigong (Babajan), which reportedly dates back to the Ming dynasty. I learned about this famous set from my teacher Shifu Lo Dexu, a man of incredible strength and skill.

Next in the Taoist water method is the" opening of the energy doors of the body " set neigong. Neigong stands for internal learning and is crucial for learning the incredible transformational arts of tai Chi, Bagua, and sin II.

This system continues with the advanced ensembles Union of Heaven and Earth, Body Arch Bend, and immortal high levels playing in the clouds. It is beyond the scope of this short article to describe these sets well enough to give them justice. I hope you have enjoyed this brief introduction to the Taoist water method as much as I have written.

Michael Luck

Ikigai

The Japanese Art for Finding Happiness and the
Meaning of Life

What Is Ikigai

In Japan, a large number of people have ikigai (articulated Ick-EE-guy) - motivation to jump every morning.

What is your explanation behind getting up towards the beginning of the day?

The Japanese island of Okinawa, where ikigai has its causes, should be home to the largest population of centenarians on the planet.

Could ikigai's idea increase shelf life?

Dan Buettner, creator of Blue Zones: Lessons on how to live longer from people who have lived longer, is confident to do so.

As Buettner pointed out, the idea of ikigai is not elitist for the inhabitants of Okinawa: "there probably will not yet be a word for it in each of the four blue zones, for example, Sardinia and the Nicoya Peninsula, there is a similar idea among individuals who lead a long life."

Buettner proposes to make three records: his qualities, the things he likes to do and the things that are acceptable. The cross-segment of the three registers is their ikigai.

Studies show that loss of motivation can have an awkward impact.

American mythologist and creator Joseph Campbell said, "My general recipe for my substitutes is to" follow his euphoria. "Find where he is, and don't hesitate to track him down."

"Your ikigai is at the crossroads of what you are acceptable and what you like to do," says Hector Garcia, the co-creator of Ikigai: The Japanese secret of a long and happy life. He writes: "Just as people have been greedy for objects and money since the beginning of time, many people have felt disappointed by the persistent search for money and consents and have focused on an option that could be greater than their material wealth. This has been portrayed in the long run using various words and practices, but continually pointing to the focal center of seriousness throughout everyday life."

Ikigai is considered a combination of four essential components:

What you like (From Your Enthusiasm)

What the world needs (your main goal)

What are you acceptable (your job)

Why can you get paid (your call)

Finding your ikigai is said to bring satisfaction, happiness and make you live longer.

Need to discover your ikigai? Ask for the four accompanying requests:

1. What I like?

2. How am I eligible?

3. What could I get paid right now, or something that could change in my future hustle and bustle?

4. What the world needs?

In his book Ikigai the Japanese secret of a long and happy life, Hector Garcia and Francesc Miralles break the ten guidelines that can help anyone find their ikigai.

1. Stay dynamic and don't give up

2. Give up seriousness and adopt a slower pace of life

3. Just eat until it is 80 percent full

4. Surround yourself with old friends

5. Get fit like a violin through the day to day, gentle exercise

6. Smile and recognize the people around you

7. Reconnecting with nature

8. Express your gratitude to everything that illuminates our day and makes us feel alive.

9. Living in this moment

10. Follow your ikigai

What interests you deeply can open your ikigai to follow your interest.

Pioneer of rationalist and social freedoms, Howard W Thurman said:"Don't ask what the world needs. Ask what makes you wake up and go do it. For what the world needs are the individuals who have woken up."

The problem for many people is that they cease to be interested in new encounters, that they expect responsibilities and schedules.

Their sense of the miracle begins to turn away from them.

However, you can change that, especially if you are still looking for importance and satisfaction in what you do day by day.

Albert Einstein urges us to pursue our interests. Once indicated:

"Try not to consider why you are wondering; in practice, be sure to try. Try not to emphasize what you cannot answer, and do not try to clarify what you cannot know. Interest is your explanation. Is it true that it does not surprise you when you consider the riddles of Infinity, life, the sublime structure behind the real world? In addition, this is the wonder of the human psyche—the use of its developments, ideas and recipes as devices to clarify what man sees, hears and contacts. Try to find a little more every day. They have a blessed interest."

A great model is Steve Jobs ' interest in typography, which led him to attend a seemingly useless typography course and build his structural reasonableness.

Later, this reasonableness became a core element of Apple's PCs and Apple's differentiation Center in the market.

We are brought into the curious world. Our voracious desire to learn, invent, research and study have the right to have a status similar to each other in our life.

Satisfaction quickly becomes the main need for most of us. A large number of individuals, despite all the battle to understand what they are meant to do. What makes them out. What time understands. Who brings the best of them.

"Our instinct and interest are extremely innovative internal compasses to help us associate with our ikigai" writes Hector Garcia and Francesc Miralles.

What is the only simple thing you could do or be today would it be a statement from your ikigai?

Find out and look for it with everything you have, no less not worth your limited time on planet Earth.

What's Your Goal Behind Being?

As the Japanese point out, everyone has an ikigai-what a French logic can call a reason to be. Some people have discovered their ikigai, while others are still searching, but express it within them.

Our ikigai is wrapped somewhere inside each of us, and finding it requires patient investigation. As indicated by those designed in Okinawa, the island with the largest number of centenarians on the planet, our ikigai explains that we got up in the first part of the day.

Whatever you do, don't give up!

Having a characterized ikigai certainly brings satisfaction, joy and importance to our lives. The motivation behind this book is to help you find your own and share pieces of knowledge of the Japanese way of thinking about the lasting solidity of the body, brain and soul.

One surprising thing you notice, living in Japan, is how dynamic individuals remain after their resignation. In fact, many Japanese people never stop; they continue to do what they love as long as their well-being allows.

To be honest, there is no word in Japanese that implies resignation in the sense of "leaving the workforce forever" as in English. Like Dan Buettner, a National Geographic columnist who realizes the nation well, having a reason in life is so important in Japanese culture that our retirement concept doesn't exist basically there.

The island of (almost) eternal youth

Some contemplations of life propose that a solid sense of network and an obviously characterized ikigai are as important as the largely energizing Japanese food routine, perhaps much more. The late clinical investigations of the centenarians of Okinawa and other so-called blue areas, the geographic areas in which individuals live longer, give several intriguing realities about these unprecedented people:

In addition to the fact that they live longer than the rest of the total population, they also experience the negative effects of less incessant diseases, such as malignancy and coronary heart disease; also, incendiary problems are rare.

Many of these centenarians enjoy advantageous degrees of imperative and well-being that would be incomprehensible to the elderly elsewhere.

Your blood tests reveal less free radicals (which are responsible for cell maturation) due to drinking tea and eating until your stomachs are only 80% full.

Women experience more moderate indications during menopause, and both people maintain higher levels of sex hormones until later in their daily lives.

The dementia rate is well below the global norm.

The Characters Behind Ikigai

In Japanese, ikigai consists of 生き甲斐, uniting 生き, which means "life" with 甲斐, which means "to be advantageous." 甲斐 can be separated into characters 甲, which means "defensive layer," "number one" and "be the first" (to lead to combat, climb the board as a pioneer), and 斐, which means "wonderful" or "rich" .

Although we will reflect on each of these findings throughout the book, the research obviously shows that Okinawa's approach to ikigai gives a sense of direction every day and takes on important work in its well-being and life.

The Five Blue Zones

Okinawa is in front of the platoon among the blue areas of the world. In Okinawa, women live longer and have fewer diseases than anywhere else on the planet. The five distinct zones and dissected by Dan Buettner in his book The Blue Zones are:

1. Okinawa, Japan (especially the northern part of the island). Locals eat a dietary routine rich in vegetables and tofu is usually served on small plates. Despite their way of thinking, ikigai, the moai, or affectionate meeting of peers (see Page 15), takes on an important job in their lives.

2. Sardinia, Italy (explicitly the areas of Nuoro and Ogliastra). The inhabitants of this island spend a lot on vegetables and a few glasses of wine every day. As in Okinawa, the sustainable idea of this network is another factor directly identified with lifespan.

3. Loma Linda, California. Scientists considered a meeting of Seventh-Day Adventists who are among the most lively people in the United States.

4. The Nicoya Peninsula, Costa Rica. The local population remains incredibly dynamic after ninety years; a large number of more experienced occupants of the neighborhood have no problem getting up at five and thirty hours towards the beginning of the day to work in the fields.

5. Ikaria, Greece. One of the three occupants of this island near the Bank of Turkey is over ninety years old (compared to less than 1 percent of the population in the United States), a fact that earned him the epithet "the island of long life." The nearby mystery is, by all accounts, a lifestyle dating back to 500 BC.

In the sections that follow, we will examine some factors that appear to be the keys to life and lie above the blue zones, giving an unusual consideration to Okinawa and its supposed longevity village. Initially, however, it should be remembered that three of these districts are Islands, where resources may be scarce and where networks have to help each other.

For some, helping other people can be an ikigai quite capable of keeping them alive. As indicated by the researchers who considered the five Blue Zones, the keys to life duration are eating, working, finding a reason for all everyday life (an ikigai) and establishing strong social ties, that is, having an extensive network of friends and great family relationships.

People in these networks manage their time well to reduce pressure, devour little meat or manipulated foods, and savor the moderation of liquor. They do not do demanding activities, but they move every day, go for walks and work in their vegetable nurseries. People in blue areas would rather walk than drive. Planting, which includes daily development at low power, is a practice virtually every share for all purposes.

The Truth about the Ikigai Diagram

Many people partner ikigai with the four-circle outline made by Marc Winn in 20146:

Yet, three years in the wake of making the chart, Marc uncovered reality:

"In 2014, I composed a blog entry regarding the matter of Ikigai. In that blog entry, I consolidated two ideas to make something new. Basically, I combined a Venn chart 'deliberately' with Dan Buettner's Ikigai idea, comparable to living to be more than 100. The entirety of my exertion was that I transformed a single word on a graph and shared 'another' image with the world."

Transformed single word on a chart? What is the Venn outline intentionally that he referenced? Winn affirmed he sourced it from Andrés Zuzunaga, who initially made the realistic in Spanish two years sooner. Winn stated:

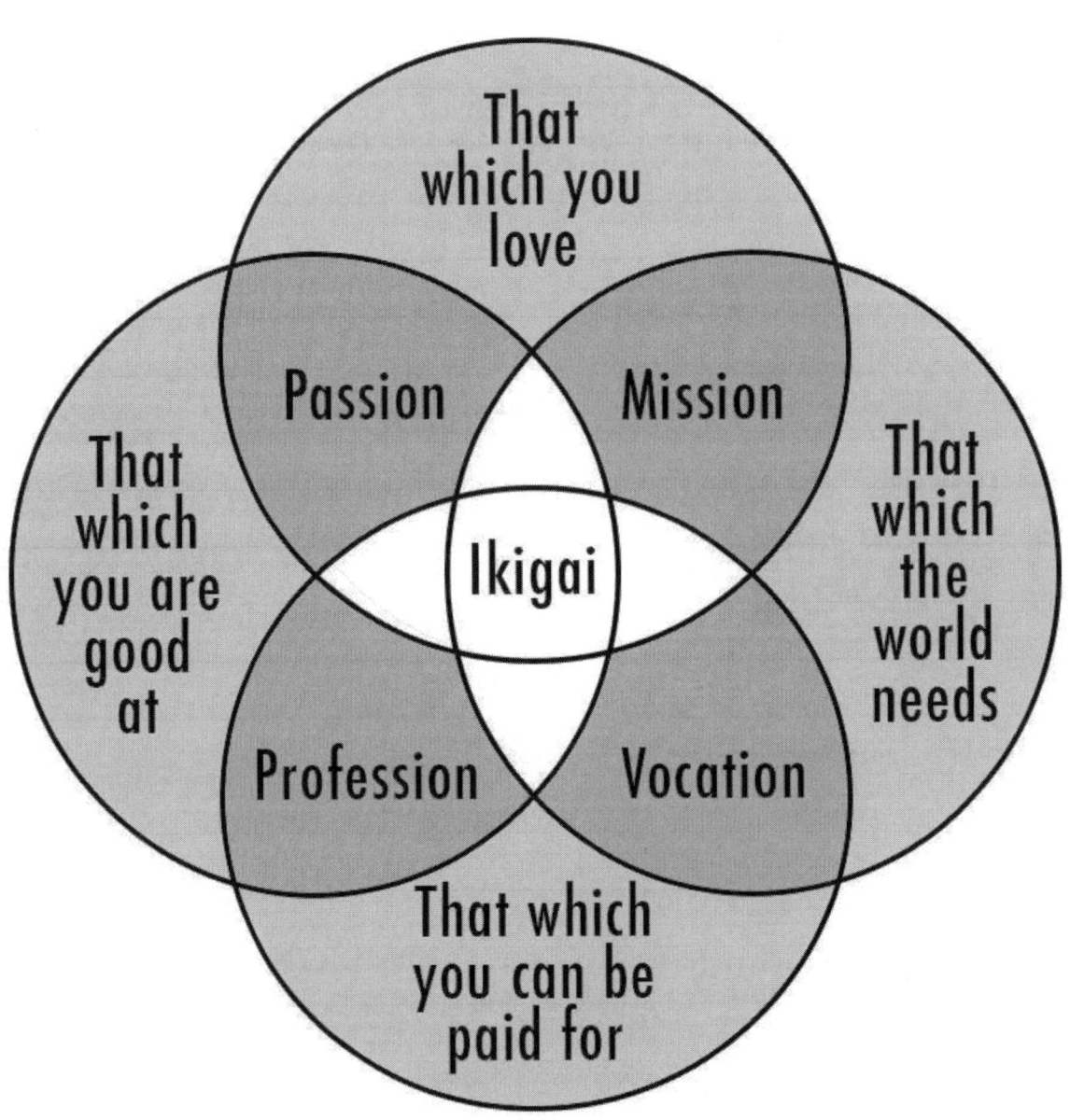

"I can affirm that throughout the long term, the group has shown this is surely the first wellspring of the Venn graph deliberately. My job was simply to combine the idea of Ikigai with this previously characterized idea of direction."

Here's Andrés Zuzunaga's motivation outline:

All in all, is Zuzunaga the first? All things considered, that is precarious as well.

The entirety of this is frightfully like the Hedgehog Concept made by Jim Collins in his book Good to Great, which was distributed in 2001.

Since distributing Good to Great, Jim Collins has refreshed the Hedgehog Concept—which was initially proposed for organizations—to apply to individuals.

I looked at the Hedgehog Concept versus Ikigai. This is what that resembles:

Ikigai versus Hedgehog Concept by Jim Collins

Given the measure of exploration Jim Collins places into his work, I wouldn't be astonished if his rendition is the most "unique" of all. Simultaneously, his work is the aftereffect of his own curating, orchestrating, and understanding get-together—all of which have affected his Hedgehog Concept. In this way, I figure we can simply reason that everything is a remix of something different.

Ikigai Myths: Addressing 3 Big Misperceptions about Ikigai in the West

1. Ikigai isn't really identified with work or cash

Ikigai isn't really about your work (you weren't destined to work).

"In a review of 2,000 Japanese people led by Central Research Services in 2010, only 31% of beneficiaries considered work as their ikigai. Somebody's incentive in life can be work — however, it is absolutely not restricted to that." — BBC

There is proof in the way that numerous Japanese individuals keep seeking after their ikigai until the finish of their lives.

"Numerous Japanese individuals never truly resign— they continue doing what they love for whatever length of time that their well-being allows."

Other than work, ikigai can be family, a fantasy, or essentially the otherworldly inclination that life merits living:

"Ikigai might be thought about either as the 'object' that causes one's life to appear to merit living (ikigai taishō)— one's work or family or dream—or as the inclination that life merits living (ikigai kan)."[1]

"The word 'ikigai' is normally used to demonstrate the wellspring of significant worth in one's life or the things that make one's life advantageous (for instance, one may state: 'This kid is my ikigai'). The word is also utilized to allude to mental and otherworldly conditions under which people feel that their lives are valuable."

This is a major contrast contrasted with different models for every reason. For example, Simon Sinek and his co-creators of Find Your Why state.

"The reality is your family isn't your WHY."

I can't help contradicting them. Rather, I concur with Oprah in her book The Path Made Clear when she says:

"Your motivation doesn't need to be attached to your vocation. I have numerous companions who revealed to me they realized they were intended to have youngsters before they even comprehended what it was to imagine. I've generally accepted that tolerating the call to be a mother is the decision to turn into a definitive otherworldly instructor. Since moms live in administration and penance to their youngsters."

Normally, on the off chance that your ikigai doesn't need to be business-related, at that point, cash can (and should) be eliminated from the graph. Alongside the discernment that ikigai identifies with work, the hover for "that which you can be paid for" gets a great deal of analysis for being a distortion by Westerners.

"Finding the appropriate responses and a harmony between these four territories could be a course to ikigai for Westerners searching for a fast understanding of this way of thinking. However, in Japan, ikigai is a more slow cycle and regularly has nothing to accomplish with work or pay." — Laura Oliver

"Ikigai gives people a feeling of a daily existence worth living. It isn't really identified with financial status. Practices which cause one to feel ikigai are not activities which people are compelled to take, yet they are unconstrained exercises which individuals attempt readily. Ikigai is close to home; it mirrors the internal identity of an individual and communicates that dependably. It builds up a novel mental world in which the individual can feel at ease."

A few, as Tim Tamashiro, accept this could be reevaluated as "what you can be compensated for."

2. Ikigai doesn't need to be seen as a mind-boggling, win or bust life reason

There's no lack of individuals out there who need to persuade you that you have one life reason and one life reason as it were. This can be inconceivably overpowering for individuals as they attempt to locate their unparalleled reason.

What I've discovered is that:

"Ikigai isn't something amazing or remarkable. It's something quite matter-of-actuality." — Gordon Mathews, teacher of anthropology

"You don't require enormous desire to be exceptionally glad; you simply need a lot of companions to drink green tea and talk with. Dispose of the wreck and at the center is your ikigai." — Héctor García

It's about the cycle versus the last point.

"I have learned in my own examination with more established Japanese, what makes ikigai successful is its inseparable connect to a feeling of authority – the

thought known as 'chantosuru' that things ought to be done appropriately. In that capacity, ikigai stresses cycle and drenching instead of a last point."
— Iza Kavedžija13

3. You can have more than one ikigai in your life

One thing to remember is that you can alter your life reason at any age. It's characteristic that your motivation will develop after some time:

"They have a significant reason throughout everyday life or a few. They have an ikigai. However, they don't pay attention to it as well. They are loose and appreciate all that they do."

What is your ikigai?

There is a specific technique to give meaning to your ikigai, which depends on the conventional Japanese culture from which the idea was conceived. It works around four queries that need to be answered in a particular request.

You can draw your Venn scheme from the converging circles of the ikigai image and detect your answers to the underlying questions in the huge outer circles. This allows you to quickly see which words appear in the contiguous or reverse parts of the graph.

What you Like

This research is related to making sense of what you discover funny, intriguing and persuasive

What could you do at random that you do not need to emphasize the money of creation?

How can you invest your energy in a long getaway or a weekend?

What is energizing for you and makes your juice flow when you do it?

What could you argue vigorously for a while?

What the World Needs

This research aims to give meaning to what it can bring to the world, its way of life, or its family.

What problems in your general public might want to help you understand right away?

What problems in your locality/everyone touches you internally?

Are people willing to leave their goods behind to buy what you sell?

Will your work apply another ten years (or even a century) from now on?

How are you Acceptable

This research aims to give meaning to his characteristic blessings: his gifts and abilities.

In which parts of your current workplace would you say it is easily acceptable?

What do you do among the best in your work environment/network (or even worldwide)?

With a little more education and experience, could you be among the best at what you do?

What You Can Pay

This question concerns things that you can put on your table, whether you like them or not.

Recently, have you been paid for what you do? Have you ever been paid for what you do? If not, are the others paid for this work?

Is it true that from now on, you will do what you do? Will you inevitably get by doing this work?

Take a few moments to compose sentences, expressions and thoughts that arise for you in each circle, how much to look for common cover territories. When you have answers to these questions, you can start looking at the different places where they converge.

Each of these components and the associations they have with each other. The idea is to have all the crossing parts in balance—directly at the focal point of the map is the solution for your ikigai, which will be your key to a prosperous, joyful, and long life.

The key to a long and joyful life is to live with a regular reason. The first step to living with a design is to regain control of his destiny, and Japanese ikigai's idea is such a brilliant tool to do it. It can take years or even decades to find its purpose behind being. However, show moderation; you deserve it.

Take care of her with everything she has as soon as time permits. Finding your ikigai is an extremely edifying cycle, and it is absolutely worth the time and effort it takes.

It is revealing that only a quarter of the idea is legitimately about work. In a Japanese overview, only 31 percent saw their business as their ikigai. Analyze this, from a nation known for work addiction, with 51 percent of Americans who said in a Pew Research Center study that their character is related to their occupations.

That is why I had no idea what was wrong with my accumulated high life; I kept seeing the results, focusing on the next. However, while composing a book may be a laudable desire, Garcia says, it is not ikigai. "It's a target. Ikigai en; I need to compose and be expected so that my thoughts can change the world."Mixing that I am acceptable and loving-communicating - with the world's needs and being paid takes me back and forth to the center.

However, you do not wake up one day with ikigai. Natural in the term is the ability to search for it effectively. To find out yours, ask yourself these questions.

When do You Normally Feel Energetic?

Consider the minutes when you feel freer and "in the flow."For one individual, this can be cultivated; for another, singing or participating in basic political support. It could be associated with your work or not in any way, says Chloe Carmichael, Ph.D., A New York therapist in private practice.

"In case you're looking for a reason at work, you have to understand the explanation that gives the reason," he says. "Is it safe to say that transmit, teach, motivate or help make an article that improves people's lives? Or, on the other hand, does your work incite something greater for the people around you, for example, by giving a home, strength and property to your family? Which can also be a source of ikigai".

What are Their Qualities?

Inspect what you consider and appreciate. It tends to be outrageously easy to get to the heart of what makes the biggest difference, says life mentor Cortney McDermott, creator of change begins in you. One thought, write the names of four people you have with great respect; it could be your mother or Opah, and five attributes for each.

"The characteristics you notice, such as consideration, tolerance or a hardworking attitude, are probably the ones you want in yourself," McDermott says. Let these qualities guide your reasoning and activities. The moment you fulfill these states, being intentionally calm when you prepare a renewed person to work, you approach your ikigai.

Can you See the Drawings?

For many people, ikigai is not static, but it grows and changes throughout life, Garcia says. "Some might find out by having young people. Over time, as young people grow up, they need to change their vitality. What remain more stable, repeating arguments, things that regularly give up and give you joy." These may require your ikigai.

Danielle Dineen, 34, has been fruitful but consumed in her industry. She began to see that her favorite minutes were happening outside of work, regularly at the party's time with partners who could reveal their problems to her. "I loved listening to people, and I was OK to convince them to open up and find ways to be more cheerful or settle down better options. See it helped her remember Central School and high school when she was the provider of recommendations to her peers."

This caused Dineen to get an ace in social work. Currently, as a specialist, he uses his listening and compassion skills (the circles "what you are acceptable" and "what you love" float) in his vocation (the circles "what the world needs" and "what can pay you"). Explosion: "ikigai."

How Ikigai Can Transform You

In Buettner's book, additionally named The Blue Zones, he portrays how individuals in Okinawa appreciate "what might be the most elevated future" on the planet.

"At the point when I was investigating that National Geographic story on life span, it was really evident that for Okinawan centenarians, ikigai was fundamental to what in particular props them up step by step. It gets them up and keeps them dynamic and drew in with the world."

Longer and Better All-Round Living

Dan focuses on measurements from other driving life span analysts, saying, "Broadly, an examination researcher called Robert Butler reflectively took a gander at seniors who could communicate their feeling of direction or their life meaning, which is a type of ikigai, and found that individuals who knew where they were going throughout everyday life – and who knew their interests and reason – lived around eight years longer than the individuals who were rudderless."

Furthermore, finding your ikigai encourages you to channel your motivation, yet also causes you to center around the more significant parts of life – smart dieting, investing energy in nature, setting aside a few minutes for loved ones, and guaranteeing you put in a safe spot suitable time for yourself.

"Individuals with a feeling of direction are the ones who are bound to turn out to be regular, eat well, take their prescriptions and keep their minds drew in, so those things will play into it too," says Dan. He features how the way of life – and not qualities – is the central determinant of how sound we are and underscores how this has a ton to do with a feeling of direction.

It Can Remove the Agony from Mondays

In Buettner's book, Dr. Makoto Suzuki, a spearheading geriatrician, is cited as saying, "An unexpected loss of an individual's customary job can measurably affect mortality. We see this, especially among instructors and police who bite the dust not long after they quit working. [They] have away of direction and generally high status. When they resign, they lose both those characteristics? I accept the converse is genuine as well. You work better on the off chance that you feel required."

It is clear through the exploration that regardless of what age you will be, you will feel more advantageous and joyful if you trust you have a reason and know where you are going throughout everyday life. Also, despite the fact that retirement is probably going to be far off for most, finding your ikigai not just permits you to locate your importance throughout everyday life except subsequently gives that feeling of realizing that you're on an excursion and progressing in the direction of something greater – in any event when you have post-end of the week blues on a Monday morning at work.

Is your activity wearing you out? Here's the reason an experience could be only the fix you need – by the individuals who know best.

It Takes the Concentration Off Funds

If there's one pressure basic to each period, it's cash. Obviously, there is a great deal of money-related concerns that didn't exist previously – the additional work expected to purchase a house, pay for instruction, or just cover tabs while still doing whatever makes you energetic.

Yet, Dan calls attention that the individuals who practice ikigai don't organize cash, and as such, don't have a ton of the everyday pressure that accompanies it. "Ikigai is at the head of their brain," he includes. "Where we may put money related objectives at the front line of our day by day exercises, they would put their interests. Money-related objectives may follow, yet they're not number one."

It Can Make You More Caring

On the off chance that purposelessness is such a risky state, at that point, what are the best following stages for those at a junction in their life? Maybe they're simply out of college, chasing for a first alumni work and not certain on the off chance that they've settled on the correct life decisions up until this point.

Dan doesn't stop for a second to reply, "I'm sure about this. As outlandish as this may sound, the best thing they can do is volunteer. Furthermore, it's been demonstrated. It takes the concentration off your own issues and gives your ikigai something to do to help other people. Regardless of whether you don't get paid, it will improve your state of mind and prosperity."

It Can Assist You with Preferring Life Away from a Telephone Screen

"The possibility of ikigai is interestingly a 'Blue Zones' idea," accentuates Dan. Blue Zones will, in general, be little regions based around network, heritage and agribusiness, where the way of life has not moved with the movement of time and innovation. So does the ascent of tech, telephones and independence in Europe and past repudiate the idea of ikigai?

To stop a long story, yes. What's more, the vast majority would lie in the event that they didn't definitely realize that web-based media accompanies addictive, stress-instigating results. "These are conventional societies, and their practices are lost in our universe of online media and TV," says Dan. He includes that as opposed to grasping various qualities and societies, the ascent of a 'me-first' society is "adding to a situation of self-centeredness that is hostile to ikigai."

In a Western reality where the normal individual is more detached from their neighbors than any other time in recent memory, online media is progressively distancing ages, different mental and financial obstacles are leaving millennial at a junction, and me-first governmental issues are on the ascent, ikigai is an expected tale; an update that you can have direction and head without acting naturally serving, and may very well be a basic advance towards carrying on with an additionally satisfying life.

Utilizing Ikigai to Characterize or Reclassify Organization's Motivation

Working in co-creation meetings, we addressed the accompanying inquiries:

#1: What you are acceptable at?

What are we acceptable at?

What are the aptitudes and gifts we have?

What do we have experience doing?

#2: What does the world need?

What things does the world (or the individuals that live in it) need?

What are the issues to be illuminated?

#3: What you love?

What do we like to do or encounter?

What are the things that fulfill us?

#4: WHY do you get paid?

What are the things with which we can procure cash?

Things we can do or make that can pay us?

When the past inquiries have been replied to, we acquire data about the organization in the accompanying perspectives:

A: Passion: The things we are acceptable at and love to do

B: Mission: The things that we love to do and that the world likewise needs.

C: Profession: The things we are acceptable at and can be paid for.

D: Vocation: The things that we can be paid for and that are likewise what the world needs

E: Ikigai: Our Ikigai is the individual crossing point of what we are acceptable at, what the world needs, what we can be paid for and what we like to do.

The reason for organizations won't just decide how they can improve the world, yet will permit their laborers to feel pleased and related to where they work. That is why it is significant that organizations characterize or reclassify their explanation behind being and be disguised all through the association.

How Ikigai Can Help Your Business Succeed

A small island off the southern coast of the main Japanese island. Some may know this from the U.S. Army and the bases there. In any case, as Japan's social service indicates, it is also known that the island has probably the most notable population of centenarians and incredibly low rates of unrest affecting the rest of today's social orders.

Why ever? In fact, many elements probably affect everything; in any case, one of the most fascinating is that the people of Okinawa have a long convention to make a paid and meaningful life for themselves. In addition, as noted by Dan Buettner, a member of the National Geographic and the most appreciated creator of the New York Times, this has led to high levels of individual happiness and satisfaction and a strong sense of direction throughout everyday life.

Okinawa residents gave a name to this general feeling of moving into an important life. The

Japanese word is ikigai (eek-EE-articulated companion) and speaks of equality between four key factors that drive success and inspiration: enthusiasm, skill, commitment and courage.

As a methodological mentor, I found that organizations can use these four equivalent components to identify an ideal parity that makes an outstanding and amazing primary impulse for an organization's development and strength. Although their application to a company is unique, the central thoughts are equivalent and produce quite well.

These are the four components of ikigai and how we can apply them to organizations to help regulate their association.

1. What are you energetic about

The first is to find and explain what really excites you. For an individual, this is what you like to do. For an organization, this is what work guides the association's lifestyle. This could be a particular action, an effect it has on the planet or a customer who likes to help.

Some models that ring a bell: Apple wants to make a good innovation, Toms Shoes wants to help networks that are unattended, and Google wants to compose the data. However, the trick is that there can be many things you like to do; only some of them also comply with the different rules below.

2. In what you are acceptable

While you can like to do a lot of things, it will be really acceptable in some of them. Also, to continue with a meaningful life and be a uniform company, you need to make sure that you are acceptable in what you are doing. This is where ikigai comes out of the normal orientation simply "do what you like," and everything else will follow. In fact, just doing what you like will not have a meaningful life. You have to be acceptable, too.

3. What the world needs

Whether or not you are an individual or a company, if what you are focusing on is usually not necessary on the planet, you will invest a ton of energy in doing things that will be unused and sloppy. Your concentrate should give an article or administration that is attractive and in demand from someone somewhere.

Although it is correct to have a specialty, you need to make sure that you have a large enough market to set up a business. Fortunately, in today's deeply associated world, you can create highly specialized markets and contact them comprehensively via the web. I am constantly surprised to meet inconceivably committed organizations that have large business sectors behind them.

4. What can you afford

While you can discover something you like, something you are acceptable and something people need, in case you don't pay enough to take care of your expenses, as well as getting a reasonable profit, it won't be exceptionally effective. The problem that your article or administration understands must be significant enough to push people to leave their deserved money behind. Otherwise, it builds a base, not a company.

Like the people of Okinawa, incredible organizations have discovered a weak point that covers each of these four components and has had access to ikigai art. In addition, as they advance and change with the world, they proceed to filter and perfect this difficult exercise.

Done inefficiently, it will result in poor quality execution and dissatisfaction. Beautifully progressed, it can make a daily existence full of importance and effect.

Find Your Ikigai By Self-Reflection

The Japanese idea Ikigai can assist you with discovering this reason and enthusiasm.

Ikigai is a blend of the words "iki,"signifying "life,"and "kai,"signifying "result," or "worth."

The thought behind ikigai is that there is something in your life or something which could turn into a piece of your life that carries an incentive to everybody and everything around you, your family, your locale, and your condition. This is your life reason, your Ikigai.

A reason-driven life resembles running on a full gas tank with every one of your attachments starting impeccably. Finding your ikigai and tailing it makes life a lot simpler and more significant. It will give you something you appreciate more than everything else during the great occasions, something to help you through the difficult situations, and something to give a sentiment of fulfillment by the day's end, letting you rest well in bed around evening time. In the first part of the day, you will be anxious to start your day. (Now and then excessively enthusiastic! I jumped up to complete this course, at that point, acknowledged it was just 3AM, LOL.)

Numerous individuals discover their Ikigai inevitably, normally unintentionally. They become a parent, land a fantasy work, begin voyaging, compose a book, discover religion, make innovation, and abruptly understand this is what they were expected to do from the start. That it is the thing that they need to live and kick the bucket for; this is their commitment to the planet and reason throughout everyday life.

A few people know since early on - a lot of instructors and specialists experience this. It's work for them, however, a calling or business. It's an inward drive and ability for other people, such as being an essayist, craftsman or artist.

Now and then, it can happen precipitously. For the majority of individuals, be that as it may, the revelation comes following quite a while of soul looking or even many years of capricious meandering. By far, most individuals won't discover their Ikigai until they are in their forties or more established, in the event that they even trouble to look.

At times this can prompt missteps in heading and undesirable responsibilities and a profound feeling of disappointment about the past. What's more, those are only the individuals who discover it. A lot more never discover their Ikigai and battle each day to discover importance in their life. They can get discouraged, reasoning that it is all trivial.

So, how would we locate our very own ikigai? To begin with, we have to begin by finding the four implications of life.

The Four Meanings of Life

These four implications are viewed as the foundations of one's Ikigai, and everything four requires to be available in differing degrees so as to be sensibly certain you have discovered your significance throughout everyday life, what the French call Raison d'être.

Be that as it may, it isn't as basic as picking something with each of the four implications. This is on the grounds that each importance should be found independently in a legitimate, intelligent way. This implies requiring some serious energy over each; Journaling can help.

With regard to these four implications, there are a few different ideas to consider.

Finding what you genuinely love, the Kondo technique forever

In the event that you have examined intentional, significant living, you have likely gone over moderation and the Kondo strategy. The Kondo technique is a method of cleaning up. You take each thing in your home and inquire about whether it really carries delight to your heart if truly, keep it. Assuming no, dispose of it.

Sell it on the web, offer it to a noble cause, discover somebody who truly cherishes it, sell it at a swap meet or yard deal, or simply leave it outside in a crate that says, "Allowed to a decent home."

Finding the things you genuinely love is a comparative methodology. Record a rundown of all that you are thankful for throughout everyday life. At that point, proceed with extreme attention to detail and ask yourself, "Would I be able to live without this?"

Normally, you can live without numerous things. In any case, if abandoning a person or thing pulls at your heart, at that point, you love it a lot to release it. In the event that you don't feel an ache, provide it up to prepare for additional things you love. (Apologies, Farmville2!)

Love is likewise the feeling for individuals, pets, etc. How does our adoration for the individuals in our lives spike us to accomplish our motivation throughout everyday life?

At that point, we have abilities. These go past simply our aptitude at work, or at playing the violin, for instance. Have you, at any point, seen that a few people are extraordinary at coexisting with others? Or, on the other hand, astounding pioneers? Or then again that a few people appear to be quiet in any event, addressing enormous groups, when a large portion of us would take cover in the background shuddering with dread?

Your ikigai can assist you with halting keeping yourself down. For instance, truly, it is unpleasant and, in any event, humiliating to get up before a group of people to give a discussion, yet figure what number of individuals you can help and move thusly.

Finding your ikigai can likewise be tied in with putting resources into yourself. Utilizing a similar model, what might it take for you to figure out how to be a superior speaker so you could help many more individuals? Practice, openings, practicing, joining Toastmasters, etc., may all approach to help your abilities. All it would require some investment and exertion, and maybe a minimal expenditure for courses to examine. The decision would be yours.

Finding what you progress admirably

We spend around 33% of our life at work. This being the situation, it's ideal to discover something you love doing that you can uphold yourself at. Having said that, it's additionally never past the point where it is possible to adjust your perspective and seek after an alternate dream, similar to the long term olds moving on from clinical school these days since they need to have any kind of effect on the planet.

In case you're not leaping up each morning anxious to begin your day and feel slow and tired constantly, here may be a befuddle between your present place of employment or vocation and your ikigai.

What are your fundamental abilities? Make an effort not to contrast yourself with others; however, concede where your actual aptitudes are, regardless of whether you are not right now utilizing them in your current activity.

Rate yourself on a scale from 1 to 10, with one being not incredible to ten being profoundly talented.

Next, position those equivalent abilities regarding the amount you appreciate them, with one being the least and ten being the most. Include your sums. Any things that scores more than 15 is one you ought to concentrate on.

Successful time the board

Keep a period log each day for seven days, isolated into brief augmentations. Shut out the time you rest. You ought to permit yourself 8 hours. That gives you another 16 to represent. Is it true that you are dealing with your time well and benefiting as much as possible from it? Or then again, would you say you are tarrying? Or then again, are time squanderers and time eaters eating up your day so that when you get around to the significant things, the workday is about finished, and you are too worn out to even think about tackling anything?

On the off chance that this seems like you, and you are investing a ton of energy in errands you truly don't care for or are not that acceptable at, it might be an ideal opportunity to assign, and additionally, figure out how to re-appropriate them.

Finding what the world needs

This part of your self-evaluation, thinking past your responsibility to find what is helpful on the planet and what is required, must correspond to what you specialize in. A few things are missing, yet not truly required. A few things are truly required, yet additionally promptly accessible.

A few things are missing, yet we can't actually give them. Notwithstanding, a portion of our blessings are required and significant aptitudes that not every person has.

Work out the elite of abilities you have, which you know to be sought after. Which ones are in the most appeal? Which do you have the most ability in?

Cost is about grace and request. Consider the current patterns in your industry and what main thrusts are grinding away. Taking advantage of these could simply be the key to your business and money related achievement.

Finding what you can benefit from so as to help yourself

This covers all potential wellsprings of business you can procure cash from. On the off chance that you haven't refreshed your resume as of late, this would be a decent spot to begin. Work out the entirety of the undertakings you perform. Use activity words, for example, oversee, regulate, etc.

Incorporate catchphrases identified with your industry. What abilities do you have? What programming have you aced that is viewed as fundamental?

When you've drafted your rundowns, go onto a site like Indeed.com and utilize several catchphrases to perceive what occupations are accessible. Utilize the postings as motivation to add different aptitudes and abilities to your resume.

Beast is another valuable site that will permit you to post your resume and go after jobs important to you. We've likewise discovered it is utilized frequently by selection representatives, so you may end up giving fascinating open doors you may not, in any case, have gotten some answers because of your key worded.

The equivalent is valid for LinkedIn. On the off chance that you don't as of now have a LinkedIn profile, set aside the effort to make one. In the event that you have one, however, it is looking somewhat dainty or has not been refreshed as of late, it will be justified, despite all the trouble to invest the energy and exertion to refresh it. Not at all like a paper continue, which should be close to 2 pages in length, your LinkedIn profile gives numbers areas to you to fill in as much as you prefer, from your past occupations and training to your distributions, abilities, good cause work, etc.

Linkedin associates you with various partners and can help open ways to new chances. Over 80% of scouts online use LinkedIn to attempt to assist them with finding the correct possibility for the positions they have to fill. Note that around 70% of employment openings are never at any point recorded. They are a piece of the shrouded activity market, where it isn't exactly what you know, yet who, or how great a fit a selection representative figures you will be for that position.

Likewise, note that around 80% of human asset supervisors and spotters will run a quest for you on Google, so make certain nothing is humiliating that may stop you from their rundown of contender for the meet. In the event that you have a genuinely basic name, do everything you can to separate yourself in the business. (Simply think about all the helpless John and Mary Smiths out there.) Otherwise, you could be decided based on another person's profile.

In the event that you do discover anything negative, attempt to dispose it on the off chance that you can. Something else, begin advancing yourself normally in a more sure light.

When you have begun glancing through occupation listings, you may discover some that truly stick out and coordinate what you are extremely enthusiastic about. At that point, it is an instance of whether to apply. Change can generally be testing; however, it tends to be justified, despite all the trouble on the off chance that you procure more cash.

Glass door is another great site to get a comprehensive perspective on what it resembles to work for a specific organization. The "fantasy work" you've been aching for could be your most exceedingly awful bad dream on the off chance that you don't lead due industriousness. Peruse the surveys, get familiar with the meeting cycle, etc., before applying. Keep in mind; a vocation needs to suit you the same amount as you need to suit them. What's more, on the off chance that you have various gifts, as we have been examining, your objective is to work for an organization that offers extraordinary open doors for individual and expert development.

As you work, what prospects and assignments cause you to feel empowered and elevated? Which causes you to feel drained and depleted? Once more, this is a decent sign that you are in the correct way with your ikigai if you are feeling increasingly satisfied and satisfied with your work. If you simply feel hauled down, you're not meeting every one of the 4 of the significant standards required.

- Love
- Ability
- Value
- Benefit/advantage

For this situation, look once more. Keep in mind, take a comprehensive perspective on the entirety of your aptitudes, connections, and objectives throughout everyday life, not exactly what you do in your activity. Is it accurate to say that you are incredible at raising money for a noble cause? Is it accurate to say that you are a "canine whisperer" who can help restore even the saddest of strays from your nearby salvage gathering? Is there something you've generally yearned to do, however, never challenged? On the off chance that you did set out to do it, how might doing it change your life?

When you have begun to coax out your feeling of self-esteem and the things you are great at and love, you can begin to spread out an activity plan. How about we look next at the four activities.

The Four Emotions

The four feelings can likewise influence how effective we are in finding our ikigai and satisfying it.

Satisfactions a blend of affection, ability, and benefit. When we accomplish something we appreciate, are acceptable at, and bring in cash from, we will feel fulfilled following full-time work. Notwithstanding, the drawback of this feeling is that you may turn out to be excessively fulfilled and remain stuck in something that doesn't generally coordinate what your actual reason in life is. You may likewise lose association with humankind subsequently.

COMFORT When we accomplish something we are acceptable at, we can bring in cash from, which is required, we will, in general, feel great and can begin to appreciate the better things in life that cash brings. In any case, cash doesn't accept satisfaction, and there can be a pestering sense that something is missing. An absence of satisfaction can cause us to feel lazier, and we wind up, making a halfhearted effort out of standard or a feeling of obligation. We sense we do not satisfy our maximum capacity, and a reason for our life is inadequate.

THRILL is the blend of benefit, use, and love. At the point when we accomplish something we can bring in cash from, which is required, and which we love, we will, in general, feel energized and anxious to get the chance to work each day. However, on the off chance that we are bad at what we do, we can begin to feel disappointed. We may likewise feel anxious and unreliable because our karma may run out, and we may get laid off if a more gifted specialist tags along.

DELIGHT.

When we accomplish something that is required, and we love, and that we are acceptable at, we feel a veritable delight in the work we do and a feeling of being associated with others. Nonetheless, on the off chance that we can't benefit from our capacities, we will battle monetarily. At times, individuals decide between affection and cash and surrender a great time request to look for comfort. If we don't deal with our cash, we may wind up subordinate upon others, and this can prompt hatred on the two sides. You can feel hesitant about not having more cash, and they can feel hesitant about getting you out on the grounds that you are not doing your fair share.

As should be obvious from these, last hardly any parts, finding your ikigai implies recognizing different factors and how they identify with your motivation throughout everyday life and the moves you make because of that reason.

Finding your ikigai may not generally be a direct way. However, a diary wherein you analyze every one of these components can give you signs and keep you on target once you have discovered it.

The Ikigai Diet

Okinawa is one of the regions in Japan that were generally influenced by World War II. Subsequently of contentions on the combat zone as well as of yearning and an absence of assets once the war finished, the normal future was not extremely high during the 1940s and 1950s. As Okinawa's recuperated from the devastation, notwithstanding, they came to be a portion of the nation's longest-living residents.

What insider facts to long life do the Japanese hold? What is it about Okinawa that makes it the most elite as far as the future?

Specialists bring up that, for a certain something, Okinawa is the main region in Japan without trains. Its occupants need to walk or cycle when not driving. Likewise, the main territory has figured out how to follow the Japanese government's suggestion of eating under ten grams of salt for each day.

Okinawa's supernatural occurrence diet

The death rate from cardiovascular ailment in Okinawa is the most minimal in Japan, and diet in all likelihood has a great deal to do with this. It is no happenstance that the "Okinawa Diet" is so regularly examined over the world at boards on sustenance.

The most concrete and broadly referred to information on diet in Okinawa originate from concentrates by Makoto Suzuki, a cardiologist at the University of the Ryukyus, who has distributed in excess of 700 logical articles on sustenance and maturing in Okinawa since 1970.

Bradley J. Willcox and D. Craig Willcox joined Makoto Suzuki's exploration group and distributed a book thought about the holy book regarding the matter, The Okinawa Program.1 They arrived at the accompanying resolutions.

Local people eat a wide assortment of nourishments, particularly vegetables. The assortment is by all accounts key. An investigation of Okinawa's centenarians indicated that they ate 206 distinct nourishments, including flavors, consistently. They ate a normal of eighteen distinct nourishments every day, a striking differentiation to the wholesome destitution of our cheap food culture.

They eat, in any event, five servings of products of the soil each day. In any event, seven kinds of foods grown from the ground are devoured by Okinawans consistently. The most straightforward approach to check if there is sufficient assortment on your table is to ensure you're "eating the rainbow." A table highlighting red peppers, carrots, spinach, cauliflower, and eggplant, for instance, offers extraordinary shading and assortment. Vegetables, potatoes, and soy items, for example, tofu are the staples of an Okinawan's eating routine. In excess of 30 percent of their everyday calories originates from vegetables.

Grains are the establishment of their eating regimen. Japanese individuals eat white rice each day, once in a while, including noodles. Rice is the essential food in Okinawa, too.

They once in a while eat sugar, and on the off chance that they do, it's an unadulterated sweetener. We passed through a few sugarcane handle each morning on our approach to Ogimi and even drank a glass of stick juice at Nakijin Castle. Close to the slow down selling the juice was a sign portraying the anticarcinogenic advantages of sugarcane.

Notwithstanding these essential dietary standards, Okinawans eat fish a normal of three times each week; dissimilar to in different pieces of Japan, the most every now and again devoured meat is pork. However, local people eat it just a single time or two times in seven days.

This way, Makoto Suzuki's examinations demonstrate the accompanying:

As a rule, Okinawans expend 33% as much sugar as the remainder of Japan's populace, which implies that desserts and chocolate are substantially less a piece of their eating routine.

They likewise eat essentially half as much salt as the remainder of Japan: 7 grams for every day, contrasted with a normal of 12.

They expend fewer calories: a normal of 1,785 every day, contrasted with 2,068 in Japan's remainder. Actually, low caloric admission is basic among the five Blue Zones.

Hara Hachi Bu

This takes us back to the 80 percent rule we referenced in the primary part, an idea referred to in Japanese as Hara Hachi Bu. It's anything but difficult to do: When you notice you're practically full, however, could have somewhat more, simply quit eating!

One simple approach to begin applying the idea of Hara HachiBu is to skip dessert.

Or then again to lessen parcel size. The thought is to even now be somewhat ravenous when you finish.

This is the reason divide size will, in general, be a lot littler in Japan than in the West. Food isn't filled in as hors d'oeuvres, fundamental courses, and treat. Rather, it's substantially more typical to see everything introduced simultaneously on little plates: one with rice, another with vegetables, a bowl of soup, and something to nibble on. Serving food on numerous little plates makes it simpler to abstain from eating excessively and encourages the changed eating routine examined toward the start of this part.

Hara Hachi Bu is an old practice. The 12th-century book on Zen Buddhism, Zazen Youjinki, suggests eating 66% as much as you would need to. Eating short of what one may need is regular among all Buddhist sanctuaries in the East. Maybe Buddhism perceived the advantages of restricting caloric admission over nine centuries prior.

All in all, eat less to live more?

Few would challenge this thought. Without taking it to the outrageous of unhealthiness, obviously, eating fewer calories than our body's request appears to build life span. The way to remaining sound while devouring fewer calories is eating nourishments with a high healthy benefit (particularly "super foods") and staying away from those that add to our general caloric admission; however, offer next to zero dietary benefits.

The calorie limitation we've been examining is one of the best approaches to add a very long time to your life. In the event that the body consistently devours enough, or too much, calories, it gets lazy and begins to wear out, exhausting critical vitality on assimilation alone.

Another advantage of calorie limitation is that it lessens levels of IGF-1 (insulin-like development factor 1) in the body. IGF-1 is a protein that assumes a critical job in the maturing cycle; it appears to be that one reason people and creatures age is an overabundance of this protein in their blood.[2]

Regardless of whether calorie limitation will broaden life expectancy in people isn't yet known. Yet, information progressively shows that moderate calorie limitation with satisfactory sustenance has an amazing defensive impact against weight, type 2 diabetes, aggravation, hypertension, and cardiovascular infection and diminishes metabolic hazard factors related tocancer.[3]

An option in contrast to keeping the 80 percent rule consistently is too quick for a couple of days every week. The 5:2 (or fasting) diet suggests two days of fasting (expending less than 500 calories) consistently and eating typically on the other five days.

Among its numerous advantages, fasting purifies the stomach related framework and permits it to rest.

15 Characteristic Cell Reinforcements Found in the Okinawan Diet

Cancer prevention agents are atoms that moderate the oxidation cycle in cells, killing the free radicals that cause harm and quicken maturing. The cell reinforcement intensity of green tea, for instance, is notable and will be examined later at a more prominent length.

Since they are wealthy in cell reinforcements and are eaten consistently in the locale, these fifteen nourishments are viewed as keys to Okinawa imperativeness:

- Tofu
- Miso
- Fish
- Carrots
- Goya (severe melon)
- Kombu (ocean kelp)
- Cabbage
- Nori (ocean growth)

- Onion
- Soy sprouts
- Hechima (cucumber-like gourd)
- Soybeans (bubbled or crude)
- Yam
- Peppers
- Sanpin-cha (jasmine tea)
- Sanpin-cha: The authoritative mixture in Okinawa

Okinawans drink more Sanpin-cha—a blend of green tea and jasmine blossoms—than some other sort of tea. The nearest estimate in the West would be the jasmine tea that typically originates from China. A recent report led by Hiroko Sho at the Okinawa Institute of Science and Technology demonstrates that jasmine tea decreases blood cholesterol levels.[4]

Sanpin-cha can be found in a wide range of Okinawa structures and is even accessible in candy machines. Notwithstanding all the cancer prevention agent advantages of green tea, it brags the advantages of jasmine, which include:

- Lessening the danger of cardiovascular failure
- Fortifying the safe framework
- Soothing pressure
- Bringing down cholesterol

Okinawans drink a normal of three cups of Sanpin-cha consistently.

It may be elusive the very same mix in the West. However, we can drink jasmine tea or even top-notch green tea.

The privileged insights of green tea

Green tea has been acknowledged for quite a long time for noteworthy therapeutic properties. Ongoing investigations have affirmed its numerous advantages and have verified the significance of this antiquated plant in the life span of the individuals who drink it frequently.

Initially from China, where it has been devoured for centuries, green tea didn't advance toward the remainder of the world until only a couple of hundreds of years back. In contrast to different teas, and because of being air-dried without aging, it holds its dynamic components even in the wake of being dried and disintegrated. It offers significant medical advantages, for example,

- Controlling cholesterol
- Bringing down glucose levels
- Improving dissemination
- Assurance against influenza (nutrient C)
- Advancing bone wellbeing (fluoride)

- Assurance against certain bacterial contaminations
- Assurance against UV harm
- Purging and diuretic impacts

White tea, with its high centralization of polyphenols, might be significantly more successful against maturing. Indeed, it is viewed as the common item with the best cancer prevention agent power on the planet—to the degree that one cup of white tea may pack a similar punch as around twelve glasses of squeezed orange.

In outline: Drinking green or white tea consistently can help us lessen the free radicals in our bodies, keeping us youthful longer.

The Incredible Shikuwasa

Shikuwasa is the organic citrus product second to none of Okinawa, and Ogimi is its biggest maker in Japan's entirety.

The organic product is incredibly acidic: It is difficult to drink shikuwasa juice without weakening it first with water. Its taste is somewhere close to that of a lime and a mandarin orange, to which it bears a family similarity.

Shikuwasas additionally contain elevated levels of nobiletin, a flavonoid wealthy in cell reinforcements.

All organic citrus products—grapefruits, oranges, lemons—are high in nobiletin;however, Okinawa's shikuwasas have forty-fold the amount of as oranges. Devouring nobiletin has been demonstrated to shield us from arteriosclerosis, malignancy, type 2 diabetes, and weight by and large.

Shikuwasas likewise contain nutrients C and B1, beta carotene, and minerals. They are utilized in numerous customary dishes, add flavor to food, and are crushed to make juice. While directing exploration at the birthday celebrations of the town's "grandparents," we were served shikuwasa cake.

The Antioxidant Canon, for Westerners

In 2010 the UK's Daily Mirror distributed top-notch of nourishments prescribed by specialists to battle maturing. Among these, nourishments promptly accessible in the West are:

Vegetables, for example, broccoli and chard, for their high centralization of water, minerals, and fiber

Sleek fish, for example, salmon, mackerel, fish, and sardines, for all the cancer prevention agents in their fat

Organic products, for example, citrus, strawberries, and apricots; they are an astounding wellspring of nutrients and help dispose of poisons from the body Berries, for example, blueberries and goji berries;

they are wealthy in phytochemical cancer prevention agents

- Dried organic products, which contain nutrients and cancer prevention agents and give you vitality
- Grains, for example, oats and wheat, which give you vitality and contain minerals
- Olive oil, for its cell reinforcement impacts that show in your skin
- Red wine, with some restraint, for its cell reinforcement and vasodilatory properties

Nourishments that ought to be disposed of are refined sugar and grains, handled heated merchandise, and arranged food sources, alongside cow's milk and every one of its subsidiaries. Following this eating routine will assist you with feeling more youthful and moderate the subordinates. Following this eating routine will assist you with feeling more youthful and moderate the cycle of untimely maturing.

Printed in Great Britain
by Amazon

35928561R00117